"*Sales Coaching Essentials* is highly practical, super easy‑ coaching in a way that you can get to grips with it fa: to help you get your salespeople to take responsibility

Jeb Blount, CEO of Sales Gravy and Au

"Without a foundation and structure for sales coaching, your team is not realizing their full potential. *Sales Coaching Essentials* is a guidebook to teach new (and refresh veteran) sales leaders build and sharpen one of their most essential tools – coaching."

Tim Wood, Sales Director, Intel Corporation

"Where Weinberg is the master of sales simplicity, Sobczak for calls, and Blount for prospecting, Hayes joins them as a master of sales coaching. Having been coached by Mark personally, I read this and got insight into how he was able to coach so effectively, regardless of the continent and ocean that separates us. Mark's perspectives and approach make this book a part of every sales manager's canon, and serves as a coaching field guide, to be referred to often, for every sales leader regardless of experience."

Kaulana Shum, Senior Sales Manager, Okta

"Seller performance is most impacted by coaching – not fancy tools, not marketing lists, not product features. Mark's book, *Sales Coaching Essentials*, has a practical and simple approach to making coaching the core focus for modern-day sales leaders. Get the results you want AND develop your people with skills that will serve them well in their careers. They will thank you."

Guilio Magni, Sales Enablement Director, Bringg

"A universal challenge today is around sales leaders who just don't spend enough time coaching their team. *Sales Coaching Essentials* will open your eyes to a new way of coaching which both empowers and keeps reps and leaders accountable for on-going learning and performance improvement. This is a must-read for any sales leader who is committed to helping their people become outstanding sales professionals!"

Bob Perkins, CEO, AA – ISP

"Mark sounds the 'call to action' for all leaders to become better coaches and lays out practical guidance you can start doing today. Your people (or team) will be happier, more engaged, and more successful as a result of your growth as a sales coach."

Jonathan Swartz, Director Azure Sales, Microsoft

"Front line managers and senior sales leaders are so entwined in operations and strategy decisions of their teams, that the coaching element is often ignored and forgotten! *Sales Coaching Essentials* captures powerful, easy, bite-sized techniques that could be incorporated easily for sales teams across industries to the maximize productivity of your teams."

Pradeepa Kolli, Head of Global SDR /
Inside Sales, at Workplace @Facebook

"Being coachable is your sales reps' inherent superpower! Knowing how to structure, organize and tap into that potential is extremely powerful. Mark has made a brilliant guide to help managers get started and take sales coaching to the next level."

Sindre Halland, CEO, SalesScreen

"Coaching sales team members is NOT optional; if you lead a sales organization, It. Is. Your. Job. Mark Hayes' brilliant new book, *Sales Coaching Essentials*, should be required reading for sales leaders and those who implement his practical wisdom will not only become better managers and mentors, but they will drive significant sales increases!"

Mike Weinberg, author of the bestsellers *New Sales: Simplified* and
Sales Management: Simplified

"Sales coaching is a skill that not enough leaders focus on developing and Mark has made it into an art. This book has done an amazing job of distilling the key lessons that every sales leader – regardless of experience level – needs to invest in for the betterment of their team. Definitely required reading for all sales leaders with good reminders, new ideas, and numerous best practices. Time and money definitely well spent! Highly recommend to all!"

Zeeshan Hafeez, Chief Revenue Officer, VeeOne Health

"Mark understands the value of a sales manager being able to coach their teams effectively. I've experienced this first-hand in my time working with Mark and have received tremendous value from implementing what is outlined in his book, *Sales Coaching Essentials*. I recommend this book to anyone exploring sales management, is new to sales management, and even to experienced sales managers who are looking to add more value to their teams through more concentrated sales coaching."

Dustin Abney, Enterprise Sales Manager U.S. East, Redgate Software

"This is the book you keep on your shelf and 'dog-ear' as a new or seasoned manager. A true sales playbook for leaders looking to drive effective teams, this helpful guide is to the point and has tips you can action immediately. Something really helpful and actionable which is a rare find among sales books today."

Ashton Williams, Senior Manager
Revenue Enablement ADA

"A very practical book that shows sales leaders how to leverage sales coaching to unlock their team's potential and drive change. Practical hands-on advice on how to use sales coaching to drive execution, develop the team and achieve targets."

Per Anders Åberg, Manager Business
Development Nordics, Salesforce

"*Sales Coaching Essentials* should be in the hands of all sales leaders to uncover, understand and unlock the potential of their teams. Mark has created a masterpiece in sales coaching techniques for application in real scenarios. Your salespeople will become autonomous in their thinking, discovering their own answers, mastering their own objections, and you will be the guide to their success. A fantastic read and truly an essential one, where author becomes Coach, and Reader becomes Leader."

Caroline McCrystal, Senior Account Manager
UK&I GTM Banking, Experian

"Coaching is a gamechanger when done well, but too often underutilized or poorly delivered in organizations. Mark clears away the fog and shows us how coaching can be a gamechanger for us. Mark starts with what it is, what it is not and makes it easy to follow… it starts with understanding. Read NOW to understand."

John Massey, EMEA Regional Business Development VP,
Commercial Sales & Channel, SAP

"For any sales leader that needs to know HOW to successfully coach and lead a sales team, this is the book. Chock-full of real world examples, templates and formats that easily walk anyone through the process of coaching a sales team to success. It's a MUST HAVE in your lexicon."

Bill Parry, Director Sales Enablement, Privitar

"When you think of the lifeblood of a sales manager you should be thinking of coaching. An essential that should never be taken for granted. Mark puts it perfectly in his new book, *Sales Coaching Essentials*. Whether you're an aspiring sales leader or a seasoned master, this should be on your shelf."

Christian Curdy, Regional Sales Director, Onfido

"Sales Managers are always trying to carve out ways to be effective. What really shifts gears is when they start to coach their people. Anyone who wants to make that shift needs to read this very helpful and hugely practical guide."

Billy Franz, Director Emerging Business & Channel,
SADA Systems

"*Sales Coaching Essentials* is a no fluff, easy to follow practical guide on sales coaching. The importance of the subject can sometimes be forgotten in the current 'no time to spare' commercial era. Mark provides a hands-on guide demystifying essential topics whilst also providing invaluable insights. Written in an easy-to-follow style it is an extremely helpful if not invaluable tool for the modern sales manager. A must-read addition to your sales toolkit."

Axel Lagerborg, VP Worldwide Sales, Sorted Group

"I have worked in sales for over 30 years and it is more than my profession, it is a passion. From my days of door to door cold calling in Dublin, to consulting on multi-million dollar ICT deals with global brand names, I have learned that top quality coaching has been key to my success. Read *Sales Coaching Essentials* and give it to your sales leaders to coach their teams. The results will be impressive and long-lasting."

Darragh Fitzgerald Selby, General Manager
Business Solutions, Digicel Jamaica

"Coaching is the single biggest performance improvement lever available to sales leaders, but, is also one of the least understood by frontline managers. Too often managers confuse coaching with performance management and the two couldn't be any more different. In *Sales Coaching Essentials*, Mark Hayes does a phenomenal job demystifying sales coaching and making it actionable for frontline managers. This is a must-read for any sales leader who is serious about unlocking the performance of their team."

Matthew Dixon, co-author of *The Challenger Sale* and
The Challenger Customer

SALES COACHING
ESSENTIALS

How to transform your sales team

mark garrett hayes

First published in Great Britain by Practical Inspiration Publishing, 2022

© Mark Garrett Hayes, 2022

The moral rights of the author have been asserted

ISBN   9781788603300 (print)
       9781788603324 (epub)
       9781788603317 (mobi)

Every effort has been made to trace copyright holders and to obtain their permission for the use of copyright material. The publisher apologizes for any errors or omissions and would be grateful if notified of any corrections that should be incorporated in future reprints or editions of this book.

Want to bulk-buy copies of this book for your team and colleagues? We can introduce case studies, customize the content and co-brand *Sales Coaching Essentials* to suit your business's needs.

Please email info@practicalinspiration.com for more details.

To Jill who gave me life
To Kate who lit up my life

Bonus material

Head over to www.salescoachr.com/sce and get your hands on free videos and bonus resources to help you master the key concepts and deepen your learning from this book.

 Here is a sample list of the videos you'll find.

Asking great questions
Running a deal review
How to properly qualify
Coaching a pipeline review
Hiring great salespeople
Finding sales talent in unexpected places
Selling with storytelling
Onboarding salespeople the right way
Designing sales training that works

...and much more

Quick start guide

Is this book for you? Check the boxes below which you agree with:

- [ ] I am concerned by the high-level of churn and the loss of key talent
- [ ] I am worried about the poor quality of deals in my team's pipeline
- [ ] I find myself jumping in to do my team's work when I should leave it to them
- [ ] I am increasingly being asked to coach, not just to manage people
- [ ] I need my new hires to get up to speed faster so they contribute to revenue
- [ ] I tend to impose solutions rather than help my people come up with their own
- [ ] I know that I need to give feedback in a way that leads to improved performance
- [ ] I need to get my team to recognize challenges and get themselves unstuck
- [ ] I feel that sales training investment is not leading to a lasting change in behavior
- [ ] I really need my salespeople to stop depending on me for solutions
- [ ] I want my salespeople to follow the sales process we have invested in
- [ ] I am determined to make my 1:1s and meetings more effective
- [ ] I need to develop new leaders as part of my succession planning
- [ ] I know that coaching will '10X' increase my personal effectiveness and career prospects
- [ ] I am convinced by the need to coach but don't yet know where to start

If you've checked several or all the boxes, read on to learn how to make sales coaching an integral and practical part of your sales leadership.

Table of contents

Foreword

More than ever, organizations like mine need to get the very best from our most important strategic resource – our people. And if there is one thing that has enabled our salespeople to perform at the highest level, it's consistent sales coaching. Whether it's in the context of sales leadership or deal reviews or territory planning or any number of other contexts, coaching helps people to think through their options, make intelligent choices and develop an essential degree of self-reliance. And that's what I expect to see in my high performers: the ability to lean into their skillset, use what they have learned and then create solutions. Or as Mark puts it in this book – the ability to uncover, understand and unlock. This is so important.

The higher up the leadership structure, the more essential coaching is and the more transformative it becomes. I have seen coaching transform (literally transform) salespeople and I'm guessing that your organization can benefit from this too. We all know that sales leaders should be coaching. Yet – right across the board – sales people never seem to get enough coaching and their leaders never seem to give enough coaching. I'm always curious as to why.

My first guess is that sales leaders feel that it's somehow complex and takes too long to learn. My second guess is that people think that they don't know where to begin. What this book shows you, is that highly-productive sales coaching is within your reach.

Sales Coaching Essentials skips over fluff and academic theory that often weighs down other books on this subject. It demonstrates how coaching can work in its most practical and easy-to-apply form: conversations. Coaching is all about conversations. As my sales leaders have confirmed to me, Mark's coaching conversations have helped us to embrace MEDDIC[1], to build value into our prospecting, and to progress and close key deals. It works. That to me is the litmus test for world-class sales coaching.

---

[1] The MEDDIC methodology was first developed at Parametric Technology Corporation (PTC) in the 1990s.

Sales Coaching Essentials shows you how you can begin to apply coaching with your salespeople to get results fast. It's digestible and it invites you to add your own ideas and come up with your next steps – just like any top-line coach would. What you have in your hand right now is a powerful toolkit that you and your sales leaders can implement. That's the first step. Today is as good a day as any to leverage sales coaching and accelerate the capability of your salespeople. So read it and apply it.

Cassi Roper, EVP Global Sales Redgate Software

Introduction

When I first worked with Frank (36), he was seven months in a senior leadership role as Director of Sales for an East Coast SaaS business. He had 122 people and they were hiring in double-digits, fast. There were quite a few challenges on his radar. In our first 'scoping' chat, we discussed three things – his 'has to-dos', his 'want to-dos' and the things which were hampering personal success.

Hands on

Frank was *hands-on*, managing a team of managers, account executives (AEs), business development representatives (BDRs) and sales development representatives (SDRs) of mixed talent and high churn. He was recruiting, onboarding and training them on a seemingly never-ending basis. His goals included building and driving a sizeable territory plan, achieving ambitious (aggressive) annual sales goals, and driving new customer acquisitions.

Workload

He had to report accurate forecasts, manage often unproductive channel partner relationships, maintain strong executive–buyer relationships, and deliver numerous presentations and much more. His *want to-dos* included building a path to his next senior role, spending time on tasks of a more strategic nature, and decreasing his involvement in tasks with low satisfaction and payback.

Overload

He really wanted to enable his people to pursue and close bigger deals and lead his team to be more self-directing and autonomous so he could develop a successor and replace himself. Yet Frank had only so much time and energy and his workload was increasing every quarter as the sales organization grew. I asked the obvious question. Where were his reps in all of this?

Unwittingly, Frank had become the sun in his own solar system. Everything revolved around Frank. His sales team had learned to depend on Frank. Remove

Frank and the team were sunk. Frank had carved out a new role for himself: *Everyone's Problem-Solver*. He was jumping into the trenches with everyone at every opportunity, even where the team knew what to do.

People came to him with customer presentations. He involved himself in individual hiring decisions and running activities which were all in the remit of his direct reports. It was taking his eye off his own ball as sales leader.

Gradually, it became clear to Frank he needed to urgently leverage the innate creativity of his managers to be accountable for their own results and to drive this accountability in turn with their teams.

> You're only as good as the capacity of your team, so if the capacity of your team is dependent on your capacity, then you have a capacity of one.
>
> Emma Maslen, VP EMEA APAC, Ping Identity

Let go to grow

Frank already knew in his heart that you have to *let go to grow*. You must step back so your people can step up. You have to give them room to try things out and learn from application. He needed to enable them to enable themselves.

To do this, he had to ensure that coaching became a way of leading not just managing. Coaching needed to become the focal point (not Frank).

Eventually, Frank was sold on coaching and he turned around both his leadership style and that of his team with significant results.

What about you?

- Does this scenario resonate with you in any way?

- Do you recognize yourself or your role in this scene?

- Do the challenges facing Frank look in any way like those facing you?

If the answer to these questions is *yes*, you're probably starting to realize that you need to integrate some element of coaching into your leadership style.

The number of people who have not experienced some form of coaching is thankfully diminishing. The number of sales leaders who are trying and applying coaching is noticeably increasing. Where do you stand?

Take a look around at the people who have recently joined your team. Your new hires are more conscious than ever of their career options and choices. People joining the workforce now (and those joining your business in the next few years) want to work where they can exercise those choices and be developed by leaders who train them, grow them and coach them.

Coaching is the way forward

Work has undergone a revolution in recent years. Gone are the days of top-down, *do-as-I-say* management. If you're running your sales team like Frank (above), you're making yourself the slowest part of the process.

Customer demands are changing in a way that makes the *leader knows best* style of leadership redundant. All decisions cannot go through you. All ideas cannot come from you.

The effective leader in you knows that coaching is the way forward

Read this first

Maybe you're thinking *Hey! Isn't coaching just 'light-touch' leadership? Isn't coaching just a flavor-of-the-month or a passing fad? Isn't the best way to get things done, just to keep telling your salespeople what to do, the way you want it done, the way you have always done it?*

The short answer is 'no'. So, what's holding you back? Here are some of the common fears and doubts expressed by sales leaders embarking on coaching for the first time.

Q: Do I have to start over?

Not at all. Coaching is something that you can learn to do, gradually switching focus away from directing or 'telling' people what to do, to letting people discover answers within themselves.

You don't have to start over. You can take things gradually as you learn what works best for you, what works best for each person and what works best for the team.

Q: Do I have to be a different person?

Nope. Coaching is a style. It is not a change of personality. It's a conscious choice to change how you lead, how you lean into the natural resourcefulness of your team and how you approach collective challenges. Think of it like changing hats.

There are times when you choose your *'here's what I need you to do now'* hat. And there are times when you want to wear your *'what do you think you should do?'* hat. Just like hats, you can switch style to suit the situation. You don't have to change who you are, but you do need to help your teams be better versions of who they are.

Q: Do I have to relinquish control?

Nope, again. You are still in charge. You are still responsible for your team's output. You are merely drawing on the deep well of capability that exists within great salespeople. You will never know what they are able to do until you let them find out for themselves.

Don't you want to find out? Of course, you do. You have invested time and energy in their development to this point, so why stop there? You don't have to do all the thinking and solving. Decide to let go just a little and let your people amaze you.

Q: Do I have to coach everyone?

No. As you look around you, you will realize that some people are *un*coachable. This is not a 'fault' and it's not necessarily bad news either. The reality is that some salespeople need hands-on 'tell-me' direction. They may believe that since you have the 'badge' of manager, that all directions and decision-making should emanate from you.

Ultimately, you should be hiring and developing people who are 'coachable'. These are self-directing, thrive in a coaching culture where they are encouraged to coach their peers and themselves, and can get themselves 'unstuck'.

The more you coach, the less you will have to 'manage'

. . . .

Q: Do I need someone to tell me to coach?

No. You can just begin. You can be curious and ask yourself some great questions right now. That's where coaching should start anyway. There is no need for ceremony. There is no need for a formal email announcing that your new way of leadership starts Monday 8.30am sharp.

Your salespeople may not notice that you have started to shift more of the burden of thinking and problem-solving to them. But they will certainly notice the results as they find themselves reflecting and coming up with answers they didn't realize they had. They will like it and they will want more from you. How do I know? That's what this book is going to show you.

Q: Do I have a choice whether to coach?

Not really. And the reasons should be clear by now. Things have changed dramatically. Your team might be working from home in your time zone or five time zones away. The new reality sees people learning to cope without the old structures of a pre-pandemic office environment.

And your job has gotten a whole lot more stressful as you juggle multiple fast-changing priorities post-COVID. You can't do everything on your own nor should you. If you haven't already, you need to start coaching your team to step up, identify challenges and create solutions. That's what your salespeople are hired to do, right?

So, let's start!

How to use this book

Part 1 gives you an overview of coaching and skills to coach: what coaching is, when it is most effective, whom to coach, where to coach and how to coach, skills you need to coach, a checklist to help you coach, the differences between training and coaching, the business case for coaching, coaching conversationally, our 3-U™ coaching model 'uncover, understand, unlock', directing vs. coaching.

Part 2 gives you opportunities to apply coaching in the context of your everyday sales conversations with your team, why these really matter, the objectives of each of these, questions to ask yourself, questions to ask your rep, the cadence with which to have these conversations, common issues to avoid, how to set these up and run them.

Part 3 gives you ideas to use coaching to get people unstuck fast, common themes where sales managers struggle or simply leap in to fix by doing rather than fix by coaching, why these issues have occurred in the first place (questions to diagnose) a master list of coaching questions, helpful resources.

Companies that believe in and apply coaching throughout their sales organization are going to see results fast. It's an exciting journey and the payoff will be significant.

Part 1

Coaching skills

Learning to use the power of coaching

As a coach, you believe that the salesperson in front of you is a resourceful professional with the ability to uncover, understand and unlock.

In this first part of the book, we are going to give you the skills to get to grips with coaching so you can accelerate the impact of your sales leadership.

What is coaching?

Let's say that you are hiring ten new sales reps. Your people will need to go through formal onboarding to familiarize themselves with your products and services, your brand, your HR policies, etc. To these people, all this information is new. You might test or assess your SDRs' knowledge to ensure that transfer of information has taken place. *This is training.*

Then, at some point, you are going to sit down with these people and get them to reflect on how they're doing and how the information they have just received can be applied by them. You might ask them how they could better prepare for the next call. You might ask how they think they are currently performing in relation to their goals. You might ask them what they can do to move a deal forward. *This is coaching.*

You need both

At the beginning of this year, I had a brief conversation with the Sales Director of an Enterprise software business, and she told me that they were looking for 'training'. Naturally, I asked which training the team had received before. It turns out they had received training each year.

Different providers and different content from each but there were:

- No new results.

- No improvement.

- No accountability.

This is of course a very expensive problem. You can keep training people, but training does not transform people.

On the other hand, coaching by its very nature ensures that people are held accountable for your investment in their new training knowledge and skill.

Salespeople need both training and coaching

· · · · · · · · · · · · · · · · · · · ·

What do your people think?

Some people view training as an interruption or necessary HR procedure to go through so they can go back to work. It's very worrying from your point of view when your people view a training program costing thousands of dollars as something that they have to do, rather than want to do. But people almost never tire of coaching when you coach the right people in the right way.

I had a chat with some frontline sales reps recently and I asked them what they thought training is and what coaching is and how each helps them. Here is a synopsis of what they said:

"Coaching is what I get when I am stuck on a deal and my boss fills in the blanks for me. He knows stuff I don't know. He doesn't always have the time."

Jennifer, Account Executive

"I think training is giving us new skills like objection-handling or negotiation. We get trainings from a local training company in the city. Sometimes HR run trainings but it's usually Sales Enablement."

Shilpa, BDR Manager

> "My manager asks me deep questions. She tries not to give me the answer even when I think she wants to. It kind of makes me think for myself but I don't always know the answer. That's when she tells me she's coaching me."
>
> Kevin, Sales Manager

Simple definitions

Let's make things simple by giving you two easy and straightforward definitions so you can keep them in mind as you read the rest of this book.

Training is the process of imparting new information from someone with that information to someone who needs that information.

Coaching is the process of aligning existing information within someone with that person's performance objectives.

Why it matters

Does this even matter? What difference does it make to you as a sales leader whether you use the word *training* or the word *coaching*? Well, it turns out that it does matter because:

- The definition of each is different. Your need to understand how each works.

- The purpose of each is different. You need to know when to use them.

- The outcome of each is different. You need to know which results to measure.

You have received training throughout your career. When you're in the audience, you are looking at someone at the top of the room do all the work. That person is going through slideshows or worksheets. You might be taking notes, asking questions and maybe nodding your head.

Trainers do most of the talking

· · · · · · · · · · · · · · · · · · ·

When you coach, you are careful to ensure that the person being coached does most of the talking and thinking. You're there to make them work through the knowledge they have and come up with a solution for which they will be held accountable by themselves and by you.

Coaches do most of the listening

· · · · · · · · · · · · · · · · · · ·

Coaching invests in people

Training and coaching are symbiotic and needed equally. Training gives knowledge and coaching builds upon that knowledge.

Your business provides the training, but payback is that the person provides the results. Coaching ensures people take ownership of those results.

Sales coaching addresses what people can and should do with the information they already have.

Sales coaching ensures that investment in training is protected by holding people accountable for its implementation and application.

I'm very careful that people view coaching as an *investment not an interruption*.

I work with clients to ensure that coaching is positioned properly so that people look forward to it, are grateful for it and use it.

Training is to be learned, but coaching is to be earned

The sales training graveyard

Have you noticed that very often people revert to doing the same things, in fact the exact same things they were doing before they received training?

The reason is very simple. They are comfortable doing what they're doing, and they don't see the need to change.

Companies spend billions annually on sales training. Much of this information ends up in what I call the *sales training graveyard*.

It is a massive cost, particularly when there is no promise of that investment being recouped.

Frequently, management compound this mistake by stacking new training programs on top of older training programs with the result that the newer training overlaps or even contradicts the older content.

I have seen this happen again and again. The result is your salespeople naturally become confused and end up with a hotchpotch of sales techniques and confused practices.

Story from practice

While conducting pre-coaching due diligence with a prospective client this year, I discovered that the sales team had been on the receiving end of a blizzard of sales programs.

Sales leadership had just changed for the third time in five years. The older methodology was now seen as out of date, and the new Sales Director was hell-bent on introducing the exact sales training program which she had championed in her last place.

The sales team wearily resigned themselves to their fate. The rule book was about to be rewritten once more.

- New manager.

- New process.

- New headache.

We proposed doing a vox pop and talked in depth with the team to glean their assessment of what they wanted and believed they needed.

Here's what concerned them the most:

- The lack of consultation to uncover existing problems.

- The imposition of new training content.

- The total absence of coaching and support.

With careful analysis, we discovered that training was in fact not the answer. New knowledge was not the 'fix'. The approximately $168K earmarked for the new training was redirected.

Instead, efforts were concentrated on using the resources the sales team had access to. It turned out that the team had more than enough to accelerate results.

When your sales team resist new knowledge, it isn't difficult to predict the difficulties that you will have in getting them to adopt it.

That's a very expensive problem to have: to invest money in a training program which your people may fight you on and may never use.

A person trained against their will is of the same opinion still

······················

Work with what you already have

You can work with what you already have and analyze what is in place before you are tempted to invest in yet another sales training program which may or may not be needed.

Ask yourself these questions when you are considering which intervention is the most appropriate:

1. What is the task that this person needs to perform?

2. Has the team already received this information in some form?

3. Is this a 'skill' related issue or more likely a 'will' related issue?

4. Where in your sales process does this problem(s) manifest itself?

5. Is inadequate knowledge or lack of application the problem?

6. What have we used to determine the cause of underlying problems?

7. How can we measure the improvement on the back of new knowledge?

When to use which?

Both interventions work well together. Coaching best follows training and not the other way around. When working with clients, we can quickly work out where lack of knowledge (or out-of-date knowledge) is the problem.

We can quickly develop training to fill in these gaps in conjunction with in-house resources. Similarly, where we discover that behavior and mindset are the impediments, we create coaching interventions to resolve these issues.

As a rule, you will use training to transfer information to people, but getting them to use that information and generate return on investment from that information requires some form of coaching.

Training typically achieves results where you are onboarding new sales hires, where there have been changes to standard operating procedures or processes, where you are introducing new technology e.g., apps or new customer relationship management (CRM) software, and where regulations or compliance mandates new knowledge.

Coaching is appropriate where it is used to build upon existing knowledge, facilitate the embedding of new knowledge, improve performance mindset, increase confidence, build resilience, increase self-reliance and develop personal leadership.

Training is information, but coaching is transformation

. . . .

Why coach?

Imagine that you have had a coaching conversation with Marianne, who is an AE on your team. Can you see the scene in your mind's eye? Let's revisit the scene from the perspective of an invisible third party. Marianne was working on a deal which she desperately needed to close in-quarter to hit her goal.

You popped open the opportunity in the CRM. That's when you discovered a load of holes, assumptions and information gaps and decided to intervene. You could have approached this in one of two ways:

> Hey, Marianne. Got ten minutes? I've reviewed your opportunity. There are whole bunch of things we're missing if we're to get this deal over the line. Here's what I need you to do. Grab a pen!

Or

> Hey, Marianne. I'm glad you asked for ten minutes of my time to help you with your opportunity. Let's start with your assessment. Where do you need a different perspective so that you can advance this and hit your goal?

Which approach did you take?

- Did you direct Marianne and tell her what to do?
- Did you invite her to give her assessment of the problems?
- Did you help her explore her options?
- Was this a dialogue or was it more of a monologue?
- Were you doing all the talking?
- Were you helping Marianne to find her own answers?

Be honest. You were tempted to tell her exactly how to open her next follow-up call with her prospect. *And you nearly did, right?* And why not? It would be quicker. Less work.

And then both of you could get on with the rest of your morning. Marianne still had five more calls lined up before lunch and you had another meeting to go to plus three key-deal reviews with other AEs to prepare for.

You glanced at your watch. It was killing you not to give Marianne the answers. But you resisted the temptation to pull the solution out of your magic sales manager's hat... just like you've seen people do a hundred times before. Instead, you held back. You asked some insightful questions and showed real curiosity.

- *So, what's the cost to your prospect of having this problem, Marianne?*

- *What's your plan to help them build a metric-driven business case?*

- *Walk me through the conversations you think you need to have.*

- *When you next meet your Champion what will you get them to share?*

- *What do you need to gather to ensure we can add measurable value?*

- *Describe to me how you plan to influence their decision-making criteria.*

Marianne hesitated a little. Pausing first, she gave some cautious responses to your thoughtful questions. Slowly, she realized the nub of the problem and came up with possible solutions.

You ensured ownership remained on your rep's side of the table.

What you did:

- You showed genuine interest.

- You asked questions.

- You probed.

- You listened actively.

- You paraphrased (repeated) what you heard using Marianne's exact words.

- You challenged.

- You left plenty of pauses.

- You let her do most of the talking.

- You dominated the listening.

- You guided the process of discovery.

- You helped her call out next steps.

What you didn't do:

- You didn't focus on the voice in your head.

- You didn't edit Marianne's answers.

- You didn't impose your ideas on her opportunities.

- You didn't front-load your questions.

- You didn't put your spin on things.

- You didn't over-ride Marianne's decision-making.

- You didn't overlay how you'd do it differently.

- You didn't seek to short-circuit her creativity process.

- You didn't let the conversation end without agreed actions.

Instead, Marianne was given *conversational space* to walk herself through the options she didn't realize she had until you helped her to identify them. In Marianne's mind, this was a hell of a different experience compared to the last manager that Marianne had. In fact, it was like a breath of fresh air.

Slightly terrifying but refreshing. Marianne was being encouraged to *think* and to come up with her *own* solution to her *own* challenge. *Why are other managers not like this?*, she asked herself.

As Marianne talked and wrote her ideas down with your encouragement, she felt confident enough to describe out loud the one thing that you were going to tell her but didn't.

As you watched Marianne uncover, understand and unlock, you felt a surge of relief as a virtual lightbulb lit up over her head. (And Marianne felt no small degree of pride too.)

> That's it! She's got it! That's a solid plan. She's got clear next steps and she came up with them with a little assistance from me…

- Her prospect.

- Her opportunity.

- Her responsibility.

- Her mental effort.

- Her analysis.

- Her ideas.

- Her reasons.

- Her choices.

- Her solution.

- Her plan.

- Her way forward.

All with steady guidance from you. Great job, coach! Helping sales reps like Marianne to *uncover* their roadblocks, *understand* their problems then *unlock* their own performance is infinitely more powerful than you being the source of all answers, right?

This is of course just a story. It does not always happen this way. (Who are we kidding?) But it closely reflects many breakthrough scenarios I've experienced in the course of coaching high-performance sales reps down the years. Here are some ways in which coaching has proven itself as an investment time and time again:

Three reasons coaching will help you

- You'll have less driving and chasing to do.

- You'll have higher quality one-to-one time.

- You'll keep responsibility on your rep's side of the table.

Three reasons coaching will help your team

- Your team will be more autonomous.

- Your team will be more self-reliant.

- Your team will be more resourceful.

Three reasons coaching will help your business

- Your business will be more profitable.

- Your business will reduce A-Player churn.

- Your business will develop quality leaders.

These are bold claims but when you as a sales leader understand the impact of coaching (rather than directing) and asking (rather than telling), you're going to revolutionize how you lead and how people want to be led by you.

The business case for coaching

Your customers' demands and needs are increasingly complex, so you need salespeople who can navigate them, understand them and solve them. You need salespeople who thrive – not just survive. You don't need mini-mes who stick slavishly to 'copy-paste' instructions.

You need fast learners, independent thinkers and problem-solvers who operate within your framework but can be trusted to make decisions for themselves. They can hold business-centric conversations, choose from a multitude of tools, and hit sales targets reliably.

Twenty-first-century sales leaders like Dan Skipp, EMEA SDR Manager at Sophos, recognize the need to be able to coach every single day. Dan's LinkedIn profile describes himself as 'Leader Learner Coach'.

Dan understands that to lead, you have to learn and to learn you have to coach. And when leaders like you start to coach, learn to coach and help others to coach, you can expect to see significant results.

What's stopping you right now?

So, if these claims are all true, why aren't sales leaders coaching their sales teams enough or more often? Or to put it another way: When you already know that competent, consistent coaching is the fast elevator to sales leadership, why do sales managers insist on taking the stairs?

Great question. Here are three plausible reasons.

Reason #1: You don't think you can coach

You naturally default to giving people an answer when you know the answer. It's instinctive. Your rep is stuck again. You know the solution. So, you tell her. Easy! But not in the long term. When you override your sales rep's innate ability to *uncover*, *understand* and *unlock* their own sales challenges, you disempower them. And that makes no sense at all.

The whole idea of hiring salespeople is that they think for themselves and produce results by themselves. For that to happen, your leadership style has to reflect this approach. If you feel that coaching is something you can't learn, you have to ask yourself whether this is true. You learned to sell. You learned to manage. So why can't you learn to coach?

Reason #2: You don't believe you have to coach

The next reason is more straightforward. Maybe you think that coaching isn't for you. You feel that it's not your job. Your job is managing, not coaching. I have lost count of the number of times that I have read team-leads' and sales managers' job descriptions which list 'coaching' as a core, role-specific competency.

It's there in black and white but coaching seems to never happen. Why? It's because their leaders don't coach. And neither do their leaders' leaders. It's cultural lip-service. As a sales professional, you've probably heard that a strong sales coaching culture develops and sustains the best of the best.

You've perhaps even experienced the results of world-class sales coaching first-hand.

But when coaching is allowed to become an *optional* activity at every level of your sales organization chart, it usually slides down the list of strategic priorities. So, when you don't have to coach (because no one else has to), you probably won't either.

Reason #3: You don't really want to coach

The third reason has to do with how you prioritize coaching. When you are juggling 14 other priorities, why spend time with people desk-side when you can get things done behind a laptop? Far quicker to give the answer than to wait for your AE/BDR/SDR to figure it out. The way you learned to lead is perhaps the way you were led in turn by your boss.

And being a boss means telling people what to do and that's what leadership means to most people. *I'm the leader. I get to make the decisions.* You resort to giving instructions and creating compliance, not creativity.

I haven't time to coach, you hear people say all the time. *Coaching takes too long*, you tell yourself. What that means is that you (and they) actually don't see the value in learning to coach and committing to developing your people. So if you really don't want to coach, you'll find reasons to avoid it.

So where do I start?

Decide you are going to coach

The English word 'decide' comes from the Latin word *dēcīdere*. That word in turn comprises two words. *De* suggests 'from' and *cidere* suggests to 'cut'.

Therefore, your decision to coach means that you cut out making excuses. You don't wait until someone hits you up on Microsoft Teams expressly asking for coaching. And you don't wait for the perfect moment to start. The best time to start coaching was possibly several weeks, months or years ago. The second-best time is now.

Decide who needs coaching

Right now, you have people who will improve in some way from your coaching them. Setting aside some time to check in with one of your AEs/BDRs/SDRs and getting them to share what's holding them back is as good a place as any.

One rep for one hour on one topic. Ask yourself what you would like to under-stand better. *Who could benefit by my willingness to ask great questions? Who most needs my support – not my solution?* Coaching can be surprisingly conversational and productive once you lead with genuine curiosity.

Decide to get better

You won't be the perfect coach. There is no such person. To paraphrase Trevor Ragan, Growth-Mindset expert and founder of the Learner Lab, you have to coach 'ugly'. So, commit here and now to screw-up, learn by doing and try better next time.

And if you think about it, that's what great leaders of people do. They create a safe space for their direct reports to learn their craft. When you allow your sales team to suck-and-get-unstuck, they're going to cut you some slack too. You're doing fine. Just keep going.

Challenge: Take one sales rep for one hour for one topic. This is a great place to start. If pressed, you can cut this down to 45 minutes. Don't tackle multiple topics and don't go in to 'fix' someone or something. Expert coaches adopt a mindset of 'appreciative enquiry'.

Taking a performance audit

The goal of coaching, mentoring, training and all other interventions is to improve the performance of your people, right? No matter which of these you choose, you have to start with an understanding of three things:

- What should performance be?

- What is performance right now?

- What can I do to close performance gaps?

You do this for each individual contributor. This is your basic performance audit. The reason we do this is to decide which of the interventions listed above is the appropriate one. Think of this as *consultative diagnosis*.

Isn't this what you want your people to do as sales professionals? You want them to consult prospects so they can understand the situation, the problem and the best solution.

With the answers to the three questions, you can create a basic coaching plan. Without these answers, you cannot know what to coach, who to coach or why to coach.

Action: Review your reps' performance so you have a clear understanding of the gaps and how coaching (if applicable) could help close those gaps.

Who to coach

This is a very important consideration. As a sales leader, you probably have a good feel for your reps' capabilities already. You've got A-Players, you've got C-Players and you've got people somewhere in the middle, true?

Your A-Players (usually) don't need a lot of attention. Perhaps a top-up now and again. Your C-Players regularly need you to tell them what to do (and possibly always will).

But you've also got B-Players who – with quality coaching from you – can make the jump from good to great. You want to coach where it's going to have them most impact, right?

Coaching the core

In *The Challenger Sale*, Matthew Dixon and Brent Adamson draw on research conducted by the CEB Sales Leadership Council. The findings appear to suggest that sales coaching has negligible impact on low performers. You can think of low performers as your C-Players.

What about your A-Players? Many managers are tempted to invest effort in coaching their top performers in the mistaken belief that this will make their best even better.

But research also suggests that top performers yield only marginal improvement when coached. They might pick up a tip or two but that seems to be it.

Interestingly, the same research demonstrates that the cohort which benefits most when coached consistently in a structured manner are your B-Players. And that's exactly what I have seen time and time again in practice.

You are probably going to see the greatest return on coaching when you invest in coaching your B-Players or core performers

....

▷|◁

Reflection: Who are my A-/B-/C-Players and how coachable are they?

....

....

....

....

....

The Sales Coach's Prayer

Lord, give me the skill to lead the people who want to be coached,

The strength to manage those who can't be coached,

And the wisdom to know the difference.

When not to coach

An effective coach asks themselves: where is coaching going to pay off the most? That to me is a key question.

Your time is your second most important asset after your people. You are kidding yourself if you believe everyone needs (or deserves) an equal investment of this time. The quicker you sort this out in your mind, the better.

Not everyone needs coaching all the time and not everyone will respond to coaching either.

I have sadly seen many promising sales managers trying in vain to *coach the uncoachable*. They use up all their leadership 'oil' trying to fix the 'squeaky wheel' of the never-improving underperformer.

If this is the approach you take:

- Your priorities won't get done.

- Your 'uncoachables' won't improve.

- Your 'coachables' won't get your attention.

You have people whom you probably wouldn't describe as *coachable*. You have people who – even with the best will in the world – are just in the wrong job. I have always, *always* tried to hire salespeople who are 'coachable'.

Not everyone on your team will benefit equally from coaching

....

So how do you know?

As a sales leader, you probably have some idea of who learns fast, who responds to feedback and who adapts to what they have learned.

You've a good feel for how your people think and how they operate.

But sometimes you just won't know who is *coachable* until you try coaching them.

To help you a little, here are three situations where coaching may not be the best fit for someone on your team.

They do not have the knowledge you are trying to leverage

Your reps do not possess or have not been given the knowledge, skills, or training which they need in the first place before they can be coached.

They do not benefit despite repeated interventions

You are coaching the same reps on the same issues repeatedly without any sign of improvement or desire to improve.

They prefer explicit command and control leadership

You must provide consistent over-the-shoulder management and check-ins to tell them what to do and how to do it.

Story from practice

Ludovic was a newly promoted EMEA Sales Director and had made a bad hire 15 months ago when he brought Bogdan on board. Bogdan had proven to be a major headache for almost the entire time he had worked there even though he was in the top drawer of sales performers. Top aptitude. Bad attitude.

He usually hit target, but Bogdan was a lone wolf. He did things his way. Ludovic thought he couldn't afford to lose Bogdan so he kind of left Bogdan to his own devices. When we drew up the list of 36 reps to coach, Ludovic had left his name until last.

Against my better judgment, I allowed Ludovic to persuade me that Bogdan would respond well to coaching. Two days in and I regretted my decision. Bogdan had no interest in reflecting on his performance or changing his approach.

He was one of these people in life who can be brought like the proverbial horse to water, but no one was going to make him take a drink. Shortly after that, Ludovic performed some mental cost–benefit analysis and concluded that *uncoachable is unworkable* and got Bogdan to move on.

Reflection: It will always be easier to help those who have a growth mindset and take every bit of insight as an opportunity to learn.

- Who on your team doesn't appear to be coachable?

- What are the signs that this is the case?

- What's your next action?

Story from practice

Svetlana was working for a software business in south London. Robin, her manager, was exasperated.

She is for the chop, he confided in me. *She has been on a performance plan for four months. I'll be letting her go at the end of the month.* I asked Robin what he had tried. It turned out that he hadn't tried very much. He gave instructions. The team sank or swam. That was it.

We chatted and I realized that Svetlana was quite task-oriented, technically minded and process-driven. But Svetlana had not been given any process to follow. Robin seemed to think that she would pick up things by osmosis or through acquiring tribal knowledge.

As Svetlana and I talked, it became clear that she had picked up loads in the past eight months but hadn't been given the coaching she needed to put it all together in a way she could leverage it.

So, I drew out the sales process as a designer might draw the blueprint of a house. Svetlana then began to join the dots in her mind. As a logical thinker, she used my questioning as the bricks to build her house until she could 'see' the sales process in way that it made sense to her.

The following afternoon, we recorded the sales team's calls to listen for improvements. One of Svetlana's discovery calls was brilliant. She followed the sales process meticulously and asked insightful questions. So much for being a 'lost cause'.

Reflection:

- Who on your team is possibly overlooked?
- What tells you that they will benefit from coaching?
- What's your next action?

Coaching the 'right' mindset

As a rule, sales coaching works best, yields the most and lasts longest when your people understand it, want it and appreciate it.

They understand it

Perhaps your people have asked you for coaching when they haven't yet had the underlying training. They might be surprised when you ask questions they can't answer. You need to enable your team to understand what coaching is, how it works and what they have to do to make it work.

They want it

When you give your rep feedback and they take what you learn and apply it, that's a great sign that they are coachable. When your rep requests more such input rather than waiting to be offered it, they are likely to be the kind of performer who will do what it takes to grow.

They appreciate it

When everyone is offered coaching, people tend to eschew it. But when your reps have to *earn* coaching, they tend to appreciate it more. This does not mean refusing to coach certain people. It simply means that you invest your time and insight in the people who recognize its worth and value it.

▷|◁

Reflection: Write names of three people who need coaching from you right now. How do you know they understand it, want it and will appreciate it?

How to coach

The next two parts of this book will give you specific opportunities to coach (Part 2) and then show you how to troubleshoot common issues (Part 3) through coaching. But before we wrap up Part 1 of this book, let's give you some of the essential skills that you need to coach.

Coaching skill 1: Asking questions

How good are you at asking questions? Do you find yourself leaning more towards asking or telling?

I'm guessing that you are naturally inclined to tell people when you have information, and you are naturally inclined to ask people when you don't have information. It's true, right?

I want you to flip this around. To succeed as a coach, you need to ask questions a lot more often than you currently do. (A lot more.)

You need to resist the temptation to give your people answers even when you know the answers.

You need to ask questions to help your people to find their own answers. This is what makes coaching so powerful.

Socrates, the Greek philosopher is known (among other things) for his style of teaching called *Socratic questioning*.

Socrates encouraged his students to learn and develop their minds through asking them questions which helped them to discover answers.

One of the benefits of this approach is that your rep may discover solutions to things that even you hadn't thought of.

Curiosity is key

I often ask clients what they think the number one quality of a salesperson is. Some respond that knowledge is key. Others suggest that confidence is vital. The list of qualities is probably long, but #1 for me is *curiosity*.

Great sales professionals ask great questions because great salespeople are *curious*. They ask questions like:

- *What have you guys already tried?*

- *How long has this been an issue?*

- *Which solution do you currently have in place?*

- *When does the steering committee meet to shortlist vendors?*

- *What's driving this need to upgrade your system?*

So, if you want your salespeople to be curious, you have to lead them by example. This means coaching them through questions in everyday situations.

When you ask your people better coaching questions, you're going to help them to ask their prospects better sales questions. Make sense?

Reflection: How can I do a better job of being curious and asking insightful questions?

....

....

....

....

....

Types of questions: information, confirmation, exploration (ICE)

Information questions: These are questions that begin with *who, what, why, where, when, how, which*, etc. You ask these when you are looking for *information.*

> You: What's the compelling event behind this prospect's need to replace their tech stack?
>
> Rep: I guess I haven't clarified that just yet.
>
> You: OK. What do you need to do in order to gauge their priorities?

Confirmation questions: These are questions that begin with phrases like *do you, have you, did you*, etc. You ask these when you are looking for *confirmation.*

> You: Did you say that you got through to Greg afternoon?
>
> Rep: Nope. I can't seem to get hold of him.
>
> You: Have you tried getting him on a different channel?

Exploration questions: These are questions that begin with *tell me, explain to me, describe to me.* You ask these questions when you are looking for *exploration.*

> You: Describe to me what you think is the challenge your prospect is facing.
>
> Rep: I think they're struggling to move to the cloud. I also think that their DBA is averse to change.
>
> You: Tell me what makes you say that...

The good news is that most sales professionals (including you) have been through some form of sales training and a constituent part of sales training is asking questions. Listen out for your reps asking *ICE questions* and coach them where needed.

Activity: Come up with several ICE questions that work for you and try them out in your next coaching conversation.

....

....

....

....

....

....

Some question dos and don'ts

Don't stack questions

> Hey, Pete. What did you ask Hamid about migration plans and have you remembered to use the template and did that work last time (and, and)…

Question stacking happens when you ask several questions at the same time, one after the other. Your rep may not know which one to answer first and probably won't answer them all. Ask one question and wait for the answer.

Don't load questions

> Do you want to try calling him and giving him this close plan template to fill in with this kind of data?

Loading questions is unfortunately all too common. We try to tell someone what to do by dressing it up as a question. Your rep may be reluctant to disagree with you and has lost ownership. Ask a question in a way that that the person you are coaching has to provide their own answer.

Don't answer your own questions

> Hey, Greg. Who can we talk to over there in procurement? Hang on. I know Lula. I'll set it up. You make it. No. Wait a sec. Leave that with me.

When you ask a question then override the person you are asking, you are disempowering them. Wait for the answer. If they struggle, you could ask them if it would help them if you made a suggestion.

Do ask because you want to understand

> What exactly are the decision-criteria they're using to evaluate the PoC?

It's tempting to avoid asking questions in case they show you don't know the answer. You don't have to know all the answers. Great leaders are authentically vulnerable. It's OK not to know. So, ask if you don't.

Do ask questions because you want your rep to realize

> Remember the last time we renewed these guys' licences, you discovered that the decision-maker wasn't Richard. Can you remember what you did next?

You can ask questions to help your rep to realize that they already have the answer. They've been there before. They've done this before. They've got this.

Do ask questions to gain commitment

> So, Mike. It looks like there are a couple of things you've identified as action points. Which of these is a priority for you?

You are not looking to uncover issues, uncover roadblocks, then leave them on the table. You want your rep to unlock the next step. Ask for next steps. So keep them accountable. Keep responsibility on your salesperson's side of the table.

Go easy on yourself

Let's be honest with one another here. There will be times when you and I break these 'dos' and 'don'ts'.

With the best of intentions, you'll try not to load questions with your own answers, and you'll try not to stack several questions in one question, etc.

- You'll tell your reps things when you should ask them first.
- You'll jump in when you probably should slow down and step back.
- You'll intend to coach one thing and get pulled into something else.

I have tried to reflect this imperfect reality in the sample coaching conversations later in this book.

They're not perfect coaching conversations with perfect salespeople. Why?

It's because perfect salespeople and perfect conversations don't exist.

- Things will happen.
- You're human.
- It's OK.

Coaching is a chance to improve - not to perfect

Coaching skill 2: Listening

No book on coaching, sales or any kind of guide to improve communication skills for that matter would be complete without addressing the importance of listening.

You cannot communicate properly unless you are willing to ask questions and listen for the answers to those questions.

Most of us at some point, are guilty of *half-listening*. We are thinking of the next thing to say or the next thing to ask.

What is the point of asking questions as a coach if you are not prepared to listen?

You expect your people to listen to prospects, right? Do you listen to your people?

Take 3–5 seconds

When you ask a question in coaching, let your rep finish talking, then pause. I'm not talking about a one-second gap. I'm suggesting a 3–5-second gap or longer if you can. Nod your head, tilt your head, furrow your brow or do whatever else you need to do but keep listening.

You're creating space for your rep's brain to go to work and come up with the answer. If you jump in every time, you rep will come to expect that. You end up short-circuiting their creativity and you end up doing most/all of the talking. And if you're talking, you're not listening, right?

Be comfortably uncomfortable

For some people, listening is *being comfortable with being uncomfortable*. You have the urge to talk, to correct, to amend, to show how you know more than your/rep or the team does. Maybe it kills you to have to listen without interrupting. But you must listen if you wish to lead.

As the sales leader, you need to be the best listener on your team

. . . .

Action: Ask a couple of people you trust: *Hey, how good a listener am I on a scale of one to five? (Honestly!)*

Paraphrase when you listen

If you must speak, then try repeating back to your rep what they have just said. This is called paraphrasing. This gives you the chance to speak but to do so in a way that clarifies what you are hearing and proves you are listening. It also breaks up the conversation nicely and makes it a dialogue. Here are examples:

> So, Abdullah, *you mentioned that* 'Hamid is the economic-buyer' and that the 'decision rests with him'. Is that right?

> A moment ago, Simon, *I heard you use the word* 'trial version'. When you say, 'trial version', do I take it that you mean proof-of-concept?

> *When you say that* 'they're willing to negotiate the SLA', which part of the SLA are they referring to specifically, Sarah?

If you are listening *actively*, you should be able to quote back using the words that your rep has used. Not an 'approximation' or your version of their words but their *exact words*.

One of the worst listeners I know describes himself as a 'good listener'. And one of the most intuitive listeners I know regularly berates herself for not being a good listener. It's all very confusing. There is no such thing as the perfect listener.

Paraphrasing helps you to stay present in the coaching conversation

Action: Listen actively to one of your salespeople then summarize what they have said by using their exact words back to them. How did you do?

....

....

....

....

....

....

Coaching skill 3: Self-awareness

Coaching is a discovery process for both sides. So, take a moment after each coaching conversation to reflect. If you like, you can ask your rep(s) for feedback.

We all have blind spots. Things we don't realize we do or say. The trick is to become self-aware. If you don't know what to change or don't find out what to change, how can you ever change?

Here are three easy questions to ask after coaching to help you increase your self-awareness

- *How was that helpful?*

- *What worked well?*

- *What can I/we/you do differently next time?*

That's it. Three quick simple questions that you can ask yourself and/or the person you are coaching. Compare the answers with your own thoughts.

Conversation not interrogation

I sometimes hear sales leaders turn a coaching session into an interrogation session. When this happens, your rep might go on the defensive and dig their heels in.

This approach risks giving the conversation an *adult-child* slant where your rep feels they must explain themselves to you.

Plenty of reps have told me that they expected to be 'grilled' in their first coaching sessions. Instead, they were surprised when their coach showed genuine curiosity and gave them space to think.

Use sales coaching to find a way forward and develop a plan of action. You want your rep to think about what they can do and will do.

For this to happen, you need to focus coaching on positive outcomes. We call this *solution-centric coaching.*

Using the table below, reflect on ways to help you inject greater self-awareness into your coaching.

Poor	Good
Do I demonstrate weak listening?	Do I articulate exactly what I'm hearing?
Do I focus on process and procedure?	Do I focus on the bigger vision and end-goal?
Do I lean into weaknesses and shortcomings?	Do I lean into strengths and improvements?
Do I tend to find fault and blame?	Do I uncover progress and effort?
Do I use coaching conversations to create compliance?	Do I use coaching to harness creativity?

....

....

....

....

....

Three master coaching principles to follow

Co-operative

You want your rep to see that you are here to help them with a solution to their sales challenge. Your time is an investment in their success. It is in their interest to bring an open mind, curiosity and willingness to open up in a dialogue with you.

How can you make this happen?

Co-active

You want your rep to be as involved as you are in the process. You will guide their learning by getting them to think for themselves. They are prepared to roll up their sleeves and get stuck in. You are not here to do the work for them.

How can you make this happen?

Co-creative

You want your rep to come up with the solution. You are here to facilitate and co-create but this is their challenge to solve. Their solutions will be results that they achieve by making powerful decisions.

How can you make this happen?

Introducing the 3-U™ model

3-U SALES COACHING™

I know that you will occasionally coach people with no particular plan in mind. For example, you might stop to chat at someone's desk or give them a quick call online.

However, coaching is most effective when you have a structure to follow in your coaching conversations – whether planned or unplanned.

So, let's keep things simple with a simple three-step model you can use in every conversation you have from now on as a sales leader.

Effective sales managers coach their salespeople by keeping 'U' at the centre of their coaching conversation. To do this, they use a guided process or structure every time.

1. Uncover.
2. Understand.
3. Unlock.

This simple 3-U™ coaching model allows you as a sales leader to accompany your salespeople on their journey of solution-discovery.

1. You help your salesperson *uncover* the issue.
2. You help them *understand* why it's happened.
3. You help them to *unlock* their next actions.

Let's now look at an example of this being applied in a coaching conversation.

Step 1: Uncover

Evan was an AE with an established SaaS company in Austin. His boss Rob was on the verge of giving him the *heave-ho* for persistent underperformance.

Rob was convinced that after eight months, he had been patient enough with Evan. It was time to measure up or move along and give someone else the chance to bat.

The problem was neither activity nor attitude. It was results. It seemed to have passed Evan by that working hard wasn't going to guarantee him a place at the table for much longer. He needed to land better opportunities.

We chatted for a while and Evan impressed me with his technical knowledge. He knew the solution portfolio from top to bottom and inside out. He could talk to anyone about the technology, so I asked him non-tech questions, such as:

- *How do you approach conversations with the C-suite?*

- *How comfortable are you taking to non-technical people?*

- *How do you navigate the buyer organization?*

Evan struggled to answer. Evan was gravitating to having technical conversations with technical people in the prospect's organization. But these people were not the ones with the green pen or the red pen.

They were not the people to create discretionary budget and to sign off on initiatives such as Evan's and they never would be. Having uncovered the issue, we now needed to understand why this was the case.

Step 2: Understand

When Evan could engage with technical people, he would convince himself he was making progress. But he was reluctant to go outside of his comfort zone.

He avoided conversations with the C-suite, preferring instead to do a deep-dive into data-masking and disaster-recovery. This was his forte. His natural strength. So, I needed him to realize the implication of this approach.

- What was his strategy to connect with people who didn't 'talk tech'?

- What was stopping him from speaking to different buying personas?

- Who did he believe made actual buying decisions?

As we talked more and more, I had the chance to paraphrase to Evan what he was saying. Quickly enough, a fear about being *found out* emerged.

He was profoundly uncomfortable with the idea of having conversations with people who use terms like *EBITDA*, *OpEx* and *CapEx*. Evan told me that he felt people who used these words were speaking a foreign language.

Evan hadn't been to business school like some of the grads around him. It was a major bugbear. But instead of using this as a motivation to fill in the skills gap, it sent him in the wrong direction. He was determined to outshine everyone in the team by becoming a tech expert.

But what did he think pre-sales were there to do? What did he think that his job as a salesperson was? How was he going to close unless he was speaking to decision-makers with the power to say yes to his proposals. How was he going to hit target unless he could get deals over the line?

Gradually, Evan understood the personal implication of not changing course.

Step 3: Unlock

Over the course of a few days, Evan reflected on the buyer personas he had to communicate with. He fleshed out the kinds of conversations he would need to have to uncover value at different levels of the buying organization.

Taking the time to ascertain value 'above the power line' was going to be a new challenge for him. He admitted that continuing to prospect at the wrong levels was costing his employer and him personally.

Evan came up with a plan to step into the minds of key stakeholders. He sought them out and captured their language, understanding their concerns and points-of-value.

- *How did board members make strategic decisions?*

- *What were the metrics that moved the needle for them?*

- *Who were the economic buyers he needed to engage with?*

He signed up for online summits. He did his best to understand the concerns and goals of decision-makers. He learned to lead with insight, not to lead with technology.

He worked developing business-centric conversations, not just technical ones. And he leaned into navigating the prospect organization at the right levels, not just familiar ones.

It wasn't easy but over the next 11 weeks, Evan kept his job by better understanding the jobs of significant others.

Two different conversations

We're making progress. Good work so far!

To build on what we have learned, let's analyze an imaginary conversation with Evan. We'll compare two different approaches.

In conversation A, you are going to take more of a 'manager' approach where you do most of the talking and impose your solution on Evan.

In conversation B, you are going to take a 'coach' approach by doing most of the listening and allowing Evan to come up with his own answers.

In each example, you will see a transcript of the dialogue on the left and analysis of the conversation on the right. OK?

Conversation A: Average

Conversation	Coaching analysis
You: Hey, Evan. What's going on?	*Brief, non-specific greeting. No stated purpose or respectful query as to whether now is a good time to speak.*
Evan: Uuuhh, it's all good.	*Cursory response. No clarity with regards to the reason for the conversation. Perhaps he feels like he's been ambushed.*
You: I just listened to your call, and it sounds like you had yet another technical conversation instead of getting through to someone who has buying authority. She sounds like a DBA [database administrator] don't you think?	*Straight into problem diagnosis without asking for Evan's collaboration. You are preaching from your storybook. You frontload the answer then ask a rhetorical question.*

Conversation	Coaching analysis
Evan: She's four years in that role. I checked out her profile on LinkedIn. I think she knows what the business needs even if her title doesn't suggest as much. I don't know.	*Evan is now on the defensive. Rather than being asked to talk through his rationale with you, he feels he has to justify his approach to you. He thinks of the first thing that makes sense to him and throws it out there.*
You: Well I do know. We've been here before. I mean what's it going to take to get the right person on the phone and validate those metrics? Business-case metrics this time; not operational metrics.	*There is no opportunity for Evan to uncover how he has arrived in this situation again. You have given him no opportunity to reflect on his approach and understand which pieces are missing. Business lingo scares the hell out of him.*
Evan: Yeah but she has budget and she said that data-masking is a hot topic for the board right now. What she wants to have is an on-prem solution that make that and DR easier.	*Evan reverts to the familiar. His technical counterpart speaks his language. If she says that they need data-masking, that's good enough for him.*
You: Hey! That's what *she* wants. What about the guys at the top? What do they want? What's going to move the needle for them? I distinctly heard her say that initiatives above the $250K waterline come out of CAPEX. You need to speak to your Champion and dig a little better this time. Did you not hear that?	*Exasperated, you ask a series of questions back-to-back without giving Evan the chance to respond. Because he doesn't know the first thing about speaking to the C-suite, he's going to run a mile in the opposite direction. To cap things off, you accuse Evan of not listening properly. Oh boy.*
Evan: Uuuhhh.	*Evan is feeling flummoxed. It's Monday. Is the rest of the week going to be as bad as this?*

Conversation	Coaching analysis
You: You need to start having business-centric conversations with people who have the power to sign the dotted line. You need to figure out the strategic initiatives that are top-of-mind. You need to find out some of these things that I'm going to write down for you. Then you need to check them off. OK?	*You are now firmly in 'boss' mode. There is no conversation, just domination. A blizzard of instructions with no input from Evan. To make matters worse, you now take over and Evan becomes a passenger in his own vehicle.*
Evan: Uuuuuh… OK.	

Conversation B: Better

Conversation	Clarification
You: Hey, Evan. It sounds like you have been making some headway recently on some of your opportunities. You suggested now was a good time to check in with you, specifically to look at that opportunity you feel the need to bounce off me. How are the kids?	*Checking that the salesperson is OK to speak. Empathetic opening with a note of encouragement to set the scene for a productive coaching session.*
Evan: Hey. Sure. Now's good. They're all great. Kids are doing well. Exams next week.	
You: Hey. That's great to hear. Can't say I'd be looking forward to exams. That must put a lot of pressure on you. Seeing as you have that discovery call coming up in 25 minutes and the kids might be home soon, let's keep this focused on what you need to get from this call for your opportunity. Cool?	*Subtly reminding Evan that this conversation is important, but customer commitments come first. Expressions such as 'what you need' and 'your opportunity' gives him control and responsibility for his decisions.*

Conversation	Clarification
Evan: OK. Thanks for the email by the way. I like the idea of coaching. I'm feeling stuck right now. Your three-step model *uncover, understand, unlock* makes sense and I think that's given me some ideas I want to share with you.	*Evan has been given a worksheet based on the 3-U™ coaching model in advance of this conversation and has agreed to use it. He has come up with ideas and is anxious to share them.*
You: So let's briefly recap. Feel free to jump in here. The purpose of this check-in is to move this opportunity forward. You feel that there are some things holding this back and you said that you have some ideas. You also used the word 'stuck' when you reached out to me on Monday. Why do you say 'stuck'?	*You are confirming Evan's appraisal of his situation and repeating Evan's exact language so that he realizes you listened and understood. Certain things are holding the opportunity (not* him*) back. You start the conversation with curiosity by referencing something he said. An easy place to begin.*
Evan: OK. So, I took on board the feedback you gave me last time. I listened to my call and read my emails and it dawned on me that I am still talking to tech people. These guys are influencers, but they aren't the people who have a discretionary budget for projects like this one.	*Evan confirms that he is receptive to the feedback you have already given him. That's a good sign. He has uncovered (step 1) what the issue is and understood (step 2) what the implication of taking this approach.*
You: OK. So, what you are saying is that the people you are speaking to aren't the people who have discretionary budgets.	*You paraphrase what Evan just said to confirm you listened. This gives him the opportunity to add to what he said or amend what he has said.*
Evan: Yup… [pause]	
You: [Pause] So who do you think you need to speak to confirm who has discretionary budget?	*You resist the temptation to give Evan the answer. Emphasis on the words 'you think' makes it clear that he must do the thinking here. You can be a sounding board, but the mental work is Evan's.*

Conversation	Clarification
Evan: What I really need is some help here to break above the power-line. I heard you coach Susanna last week on working with my Champion to get to the C-1. Do you think you can help me work on that? I think it's this guy, but I still can't think of how to open the call.	*Evan defines where he needs help specifically. He clarifies what he thinks will work or 'unlock' in this case (step 3). He tells you what he thinks is the obstacle holding him back.*
You: With the time we have, how can I help you to move forward? Your call.	*Rather than tell Evan where to start, you give Evan a choice and leave it to him to select the appropriate option. This also shows that you trust his judgment.*
Evan: Can you help me figure out the buyer persona? That way you can help me with the language. I listened to my call. Your notes helped. I still need to work on that. I feel that's going to unlock the next step for me.	*Evan makes a decision. This is a good step. He feels better now that he is in control of the process to move forward. He appreciates your faith in his choice. You can agree a check-in time with Evan to see how he got on once he has had his next call. Nice work.*
You: Sure. Let's do it.	

Nice work! You used three coaching skills throughout this conversation with Evan.

- You asked insightful questions.
- You listened actively to responses.
- You demonstrated self-awareness.

You involved Evan every step of the way and facilitated Evan's ideas so that co-creating the solution to his own sales challenge.

You demonstrated curiosity. There was no 'advice monster' (as author Michael Bungay Stanier calls it).

- No taking control.

- No telling Evan what to do.

- No 'here's what I would do in your shoes'.

You also engaged him through structured conversation using the 3-U™ model and this helped Evan to do the work.

- Evan uncovered the issues.

- Evan understood their cause and consequence.

- Evan unlocked his own solution.

Part 1 wrap up

What we've covered

- What sales coaching is.

- Which skills you need.

- Where you can make a powerful difference.

What to do now

- Get excited about the value of coaching to you and your team.

- Ask yourself which skills you need to acquire and develop.

- Plan and prepare for your first coaching conversation.

Part 2

Coaching proactively

Using coaching in everyday meetings

In Part 2 of this book, we'll look at the kinds of sales meetings and sales conversations that you are already having with your team as a sales leader.

These are opportunities where you can apply your coaching immediately to get results quickly.

Coaching the one-to-one

What is the one-to-one?

The other reviews outlined in this chapter tend to be quite specific. Call reviews focus on calls, and pipeline reviews focus on pipeline, etc.

One-to-ones are the placeholder for almost everything else. They ensure that you are coaching to address what is going on *at that moment*.

They can be unscheduled 'water-cooler' moments, casual catch-ups, or more likely, structured check-ins to follow up on key performance indicators (KPIs), meetings, prospecting etc.

How does coaching one-to-ones help you?

They keep you in touch

Many sales leaders make the mistake of becoming keyboard warriors. Your one-to-ones gives you empathetic connection with the people you coach.

They keep you informed

Remote working means more and more people are out of sight and out of mind. A regular one to one helps you find out what's working and what's not.

They keep your people on track

Your insight and leadership is especially important to help your people to remove obstacles and keep people doing what they do best: selling.

Reflection: How can regular one-to-ones help you in other ways?

....

....

....

....

....

....

The one-to-one as a coaching opportunity

You can help your team to uncover, understand and unlock their own performance when you make time for regular one-to-one coaching conversation.

- You hadn't planned to have a conversation with Jean this morning, but you grabbed ten minutes and asked some great questions which got her 'unstuck'.

- You had a 20-minute one-to-one with Pedro. You went asked him to reflect on his commitments for the week. He's now focused on a call with his Champion.

Coaching the one-to-one is a chance to explore:

- Performance against agreed KPIs.

- Preparation for upcoming meetings.

- Prospecting and diary management, etc.

Your salesperson is walking you through things like:

- Where they are focusing their attention.

- Where they are stuck and need some help.

- What their priorities are for the week/month/quarter.

Not everyone will need the same amount of time with you. New hires often need more than experienced salespeople. But it's quite subjective.

You are helping the rep to think for themselves and to develop a degree of self-reliance and autonomy. But you're also providing a lifeline if they need it.

You keep your promise

A previous manager of mine had a habit of moving them, postponing them and cancelling them. But not you.

As coach, you know the value of gaining commitment *from your people* and keeping your commitment *to your people*.

Story from practice

Isman was a new BDR over in Singapore. You hired him online and hadn't met yet, but onboarding had gone well. He appeared to be settling in.

You checked his calendar yesterday and noticed that two weeks were booked with back-to-back with meetings. The next two were empty. What was going on?

- Where was the time set aside for prospecting?

- Where were the follow-up calls Isman said that he had booked?

- Where were the mentoring sessions scheduled with his team lead?

It was important that Isman got into an operating rhythm quickly so that he was set up for success in his first 100 days.

You messaged Isman and asked him to give some time to think about how he was planning his week and month.

This was going to be a chance to hear his thoughts, spot any inconsistencies and help him realize what he had to do.

You began by thanking Isman for being on time. You then asked him some helpful questions about how his time management was shaping up.

- *What are your goals for this month, Isman?*

- *Which tasks and outcomes will help you achieve them?*

- *How are you scheduling your time to support these tasks?*

The first question made Isman go quiet. He had been spending too much time on the accounts that had been given to him to help him ramp up.

- His admitted his planning was inconsistent.

- He agreed he had forgotten to set aside time for call blocks.

- He was open to your coaching so he could develop a cadence.

Isman's feedback on your one-to-one

The last place I was in, the term 'one-to-one' had a negative connotation. When you suggested that we hold a one-to-one, I was afraid I had screwed up.

I'm really glad we talked. I guess that I was really trying to impress you and the team, but I was all over the place.

My key takeaway from this is that I need to come up with goals, prioritize the activities which support those goals then make sure I stick to the plan.

I'm clear on my actions for our next one-to-one next week.

The coach's approach to the one-to-one

Average looks like this	Coaching looks like this
Holds one-to-ones infrequently or too often.	Holds one-to-ones with the team in accordance with each rep's needs.
Jumps from item to item confusing the salesperson.	Sticks to a plan to maximize productivity in the time available.
Approaches the one-to-one with no structure or preparation.	Reviews the CRM, reporting, tools and leverages metrics and data.
Dominates the talking and wraps up with no call to action.	Dominates the listening and gets the salesperson to commit to key actions.
Forgets to follow-up after each one-to-one to ensure progress.	Asks salesperson to email key objectives to be followed up at the next one-to-one.

Some things to think about

* How would I grade the quality of our relationship?

* What are my salesperson's goals and what motivates them?

* How can I align my goals with them?

- Where might I have concerns and how am I going to address them?

- How can I ring-fence this meeting and minimize distractions?

Coaching plan – preparation, conversation, application

Preparation – some things to ask yourself before you coach:

- What's the one thing I want clarity on today/this morning?

- Which metrics, activities, KPIs should I be digging into?

- Which roadblocks might surface and what can I do to clear the way?

▷|◁

Reflection: What else do you need to do to make this meeting a success?

....

....

....

....

....

....

Conversation – some questions you can ask your rep in coaching:

- *Where do you need help to fix this?*

- *What are your options?*

- *When's your next meeting?*

- *What are you top three priorities this week?*

- *Where is this deal in the sales process?*

- *How will you progress it to the next stage?*

- *What are the risks in your current pipeline?*

- *How are you tracking to KPIs this week?*

- *Where can I support you on this opportunity?*

- *What is your forecast for this quarter?*

- *What are your thoughts about your aged opportunities?*

- *What else is top-of-mind?*

Activity: Come up with three more coaching questions you can ask here to suit the purpose of your one-to-one. Which questions produce results for you?

....

....

....

....

....

....

Application – next steps:

- What are your rep's agreed next steps?

- How will you keep them accountable?

- When do you expect to follow up with them?

....

....

....

....

....

....

....

Coaching the deal review

What is the deal review?

A deal review is your chance to get your rep to walk you through the 'story' of a specific opportunity in their pipeline in a conversational manner from beginning to end.

You are sense-checking how they qualified this opportunity as well as their plan to get a win.

Of all the reviews you coach, this is where the rubber meets the road. You need to get your rep to go through a specific opportunity with you at a granular level.

Why does it matter?

It's a chance to x-ray a specific deal

You want to make sure that your rep has thought through which things might throw a *spanner in the works* and what the plan is to deal with such issues before they arise.

It's a taster of the quality of the deals that your rep thinks will close

If an opportunity is in a perilous state and is full of holes, it should force you to ask yourself about the quality of their other opportunities. Which other deals are in this state?

It's a signal to you that your rep has grasped the fundamentals

They know how to build deals which have a likelihood of closing. Coaching the deal review will help you to confirm that they are prospecting, selling, and closing the right way.

Deal review as a coaching opportunity

If you think about it, a deal review is a 'mini-story' of:

- What your rep is selling.

- How your rep is selling.

- Whom they are selling it to.

- Why the buyer is buying it.

- What the plan is to close it.

When you coach the deal review you are getting your sales rep to tell the *compelling story* of the deal rather than just regurgitate facts and figures to you.

Your salesperson is walking you through things like:

- What they are doing to flesh out the pain they are solving.

- Which metrics/numbers they have gathered.

- Who the 'economic buyer'/decision-maker is.

- What the organizational decision process is.

- How they've validated the information gathered, etc.

In this coaching session, you are helping the rep to uncover gaps, so they plan a series of next steps.

Ideally, you as the coach will follow up and keep them accountable for these steps.

Story from practice

You recently ran through several of Angela's deals in the CRM. You prioritized three of them and asked Angela to select which one she wanted help with for this deal review.

Angela selected a $290K opportunity with a Mid-West logistics company. She was super-confident that this was going to close. Only two months away and all looked well. Despite initial resistance to the idea, Angela realized that you were not trying to take over.

You were inviting Angela to share the story of *her* deal. Not to check up on her but to help her sense-check that she was adding value, talking to the right people and building a clear path for success.

There were 20 working days until the new business year when the client had fresh budget and you wanted to ensure that Angela was in sync in this closing motion. You asked Angela some insightful questions:

- *What's your plan to keep control of this rather than 'hoping' it progresses?*

- *What's your Champion doing to help you get this over the line?*

- *How can you keep adding value and stay top-of-mind until this is signed?*

Angela suspected that you already knew the answers to many of those questions. But if you did, you managed to hold them back.

You allowed Angela to guide you through the deal, listening intently and occasionally reflecting what she said.

As Angela talked things through, she began to realize that there was still some considerable work to do. For example:

- Some of the metrics had not been validated yet or tied back to a business case.

- She wasn't working closely enough with her Champion.

- She had handed over control and needed to get back in the driver's seat.

Where it was helpful, you shared your experience from similar deals. This indirect feedback gave Angela some useful ideas. But her next steps were up to her. She owned this.

At the end of the review, Angela had solidified her *three whys* into a refreshed business case that made business sense and would strongly resonate with her prospects.

- Why us?

- Why this?

- Why now?

Angela's feedback to you as her coach

It was tough at times. I felt like I should have spotted some of these things myself. But I am glad that I had a second set of eyeballs on this deal.

There were things that I did not notice and things I wouldn't have seen without fresh perspective.

I'm now clear on what needs to be done and how I am going to make this deal happen.

The coach's approach to the deal review

Average looks like this	Coaching looks like this
Dictates which deal to review.	Empowers rep to decide which opportunity to review.
Takes over the deal review process.	Encourages rep to walk them through deal.
Identifies missing information and gives it to the rep.	Allows rep to discover gaps/ assumptions first.

| Tells rep which steps to take to solidify the deal. | Gets rep to come up with their own insight and plan forward. |
| Uses their own expertise to influence the deal plan. | Coaches within deal qualification framework. |

Coaching plan – preparation, conversation, application

Preparation – some things before you coach:

- Which stage is this opportunity at in your CRM?

- Where are the assumptions, gaps, errors, risks?

- Who has your salesperson been talking to/not talking to?

- Review the deal using MEDDIC/BANT, etc. (see below).

▷|◁

Reflection: What else do you need to gather at this stage of the deal review?

....

....

....

....

....

....

Conversation – questions you can ask your rep in coaching:

- What is the burning platform/compelling need/business case?
- What is the consequence of doing nothing?
- What are the *three whys*? Why this solution? Why us? Why now?
- What is the 'pain' this prospect is facing and what is stopping them?
- What tells you this is a challenge/opportunity worth solving right now?
- What tells you we can solve this as well as the competition?
- If you x-ray this, where are the cracks you currently cannot see?
- How have you validated information you have gathered from the prospect?
- Who are you talking to? Who haven't you talked to? Who should you be talking to?
- Which are the things that will stop you from closing this deal?
- How well do you understand decision criteria and our ability to influence?
- Who else is the prospect to us and how do we rank against them?
- What is your plan to shorten the sales-cycle/accelerate through the gates?

Activity: Come up with three more coaching questions you can ask here.

....

....

....

....

....

Application – next steps:

- What are your rep's agreed next steps?

- How will you keep them accountable?

- When do you expect to follow up with them?

....

....

....

....

....

....

....

Pro tip

Some managers run the deal review based on their instinct. They spot things and dig into them as they find them.

As a rule, it's probably best to run a deal review using your sales process together with your qualification framework e.g., MEDDIC, BANT, SPIN, etc.

That way, everyone including all your managers are coaching the same way. Let's take MEDDIC as an example.

If you are coaching a deal review in early stages, think *don't drop the MIC*:

M – Metrics

I – Implicated pain

C – Champion.

And when you are coaching the deal in the closing motion, you can focus on the rest of the letters in the acronym:

D – Decision process

D – Decision criteria

E – Economic buyer.

Pro tip

Most sales managers run deal reviews looking at live deals but there is huge value in running reviews of past deals. Most managers don't see the value in running *retrospective* deal reviews; both *closed-won* and *closed-lost*.

This is where the learning is freshest, and the experience is the most valuable – asking why we won or why we didn't win will increase chances of winning again the next time around.

- Why did we win so we can create a winning formula?

- Why did we lose so we can win the next deal?

You want to ensure retrospective deal reviews take place. Top sports teams digest the pain of the loss to increase the appetite and hunger for the next win.

Closing ideas

- There are always gaps – there is no such thing as perfect knowledge.

- There is always risk (ask for plans to mitigate risk).

- Watch the talk-time ratio. Your rep should be doing most of the talking.

- Record the session for future playback and learning.

- Consider reviewing deals at an early stage, not just those in the closing motion.

- Probe, probe, probe – you are looking for leaks, gaps, risks, assumptions.

- Watch out for your rep not walking you through the sales process.

- Consider a drive-by review where you coach with minimum notice.

- A deal represents a number in the forecast, so lean into the numbers.

Reflection: What are your takeaways from this chapter and how will you apply them to your next deal review?

....

....

....

....

....

....

Coaching the call preview/review

If you're wondering which critical conversations your salespeople are having and how you can improve buyer–seller interaction, then coaching the call review is going to have impact fast.

You can coach your reps to plan and prepare for upcoming calls (preview). You can also debrief and review past calls for analysis and learning (review).

Coaching helps your reps increase deal velocity by ensuring they clear objectives for each call and are ready to add value in each conversation. So much time is wasted on the phone. Planning makes all the difference.

Why coach the call review?

When promising leads never seem to progress past the first point of contact or when opportunities get stuck in the pipeline, my gut instinct is to listen/observe buyer–seller communication. Coaching past or upcoming calls is essential.

It ensures that conversations are focused

Coaching the call ensures your rep is prepped and has a clear idea of why the call is justified in the context of the sales process.

It gives you the chance to create self-awareness

Listening back to interactions is a sure-fire way to create self-awareness for reps. Top sports performers always review past performance. Your salespeople should too.

It accelerates your sales process

When a rep has predefined goals and a clear plan for calls, they will ensure that each meeting is adding value to the prospect/customer and moving them through the sale process more quickly.

Planning upcoming calls

If you think about it, planning an upcoming call clarifies:

- Who your salesperson is calling.

- What they plan to achieve as a result.

- How they plan to structure the call.

- Which information they need to capture.

- Which commitments they want from the prospect.

When you coach call planning, you are helping your salesperson to imagine the conversation and *real-play* it before they jump on the call.

Your salesperson is walking you through things like:

- How they know this is the right person to engage.

- What they think are the prospect's expectations are.

- Who needs to be on the same call.

- Which questions/objections/clarifications might arise.

The call planning review is an opportunity to make sure your salespeople are *audible-ready*. Role-plays/real-plays can help your reps prepare for unexpected questions and solidify their ability to answer expected ones.

Reviewing past calls

Whenever I work with low-achieving sales teams, one of the first questions I ask is *How often do you listen to/watch past-calls?* They usually don't.

Here are some reasons why your salespeople may not make the time:

Your reps don't want to

I get it. It's understandable. You probably don't like listening to the sound of your voice. Your salespeople resist listening to or watching their past performance for the same reason.

They may cringe when they realize what they meant to say but didn't say *or* what they did say but didn't say well. They certainly don't want anyone else listening to those calls either.

Your reps don't have to

Many reps argue that listening to past calls is a waste of time when they should be focused on making new calls. No one holds them accountable for listening to their most recent interactions.

But that's like saying: *I'm too busy driving to stop for gas.* The success of your team's *future calls* is dependent on their ability to learn from *past calls*. As a sales leader, you need to make sure this happens.

Your reps don't know how to

Often reps don't know where to find recordings. More likely still, they haven't been trained to analyze them and self-coach. These days, there are numerous artificial intelligence (AI)-driven call-recording platforms.

These give you conversation-intelligence features to allow you to coach where it matters most. You can coach your rep where they dominated the conversation, talked over the prospect or failed to pick up on vital clues, etc.

There is so much coaching opportunity in listening to calls

· · · · · · · · · · · · · · · · · · · ·

Story from practice

When you took over as the new Sales Manager, you decided to take a coaching approach with Raheel, an AE who was coming up on three months in the business.

You explained how working together on planning calls and debriefing calls would help him to make better connections and build trust with prospects fast. Raheel had a call with a Head of Infrastructure and asked you for help.

- *What do you plan to get from this conversation with this guy?*

- *What do you think he can help you to achieve?*

- *How do you know that he has the authority to help you?*

You listened as Raheel explained his thinking. You paraphrased what you were hearing and asked helpful questions.

- There was no firm commitment or scheduled call in the calendar.

- Raheel had not put enough thought into planning the call.

- He had not thought through the questions he might be asked.

There were some pauses as Raheel thought about how he could open the call and make it a useful conversation to both parties.

You offered to run through a *real-play* with Raheel, which revealed that he had a lot of work to do still.

Thankfully, Raheel had a few *aha* moments and came up with some of his own clear ideas to make his call a success.

Raheel's feedback to you as his coach

Listening to my own calls is still uncomfortable but it's helping me. I am now clear on how to review a call by myself first before I bring a call to you.

Running my call structure past you showed me that I was nowhere near ready. With hindsight, I would have made a mess of the call without your questions first.

I don't feel so bad now when you coach me on call planning and call reviews. I don't feel I am being judged. You are creating the environment for me to learn.

The coach's approach to the call review

Average looks like this	Coaching looks like this
Finds things in the call to correct.	Catches reps doing things right and encourages.
Holds call reviews on a one-to-one basis only.	Uses call reviews as basis for group-learning.
Decides unilaterally which calls to review.	Gives reps autonomy in choosing calls.
Does not listen to the calls in advance.	Invests time in highlighting areas for development.
Ambushes the rep with the call recording.	Gives tools/worksheet to help them grade their call.

Coaching plan – preparation, conversation, application

Preparation – things to consider before you coach call reviews:

- Make it a requirement that reps listen to a minimum of five calls a week.

- Ask them to select a call they liked as well as one they want help with.

- Listen to a sample of the calls for timestamps and questions to ask.

▷|◁

Reflection: What else do you need to gather at this stage of the call review?

....

....

....

....

....

....

Conversation – questions you can ask your rep (reviewing past calls):

- What was the purpose of making this call?
- How well did you prepare for this call?
- How well did you relate to the gatekeeper?
- How well did you clarify the objective of this call?
- How well did you open this call?
- How well did you engage with the prospect?
- How well did you follow the sales script/process?
- How well did you control the next step?
- How would you do this call differently next time?
- What do you think was going through the prospect's mind?
- What do you feel you did well?
- What would you like to do differently next time?

Activity: Come up with three more coaching questions you can ask here.

....

....

....

....

....

....

Application – agreed next steps:

- What are your rep's agreed next steps?
- How will you keep them accountable?
- When do you expect to follow up with them?

....

....

....

....

....

....

Pro tip

If you discover a great call, make a point of sharing it (e.g., on Slack). This can help to correct any perception that call reviews are purely corrective in nature.

They're a great opportunity to catch your rep doing something right and to celebrate it.

That's especially important when you are coaching them on the learnings from a critical conversation with a prospect.

Pro tip

Even if you don't have a quota, you might want to consider taking to the phones now and again, so your sales team sees you and hears you in *sales mode*.

1. You are a sales leader, but you are never *above* prospecting.
2. Your team sees you as someone who knows what it's like to be in the trenches.
3. You can ask the team for feedback which makes you human and coachable.

Pro tip

You don't want any beliefs taking hold that there is such a thing as a perfect call. When reps feel that each call must be *grade A1*, you unwittingly manufacture fear of picking up the telephone.

You don't want to create the false belief that every call has to be A1. It's hard enough hearing 'no' 200+ times a week without having to do it flawlessly every time.

Dialling and prospecting is a messy business. We need to coach our people to see it as a *best-effort activity* not *best-every-time activity*.

Closing ideas

- Run a lunch-and-learn activity where reps agree to do a post-call analysis.

- Give your reps a template to use so they can review calls on their own.

- Create a competition so reps are encouraged to submit their best calls.

- Use role-plays selectively so people aren't embarrassed or self-conscious.

- Leverage AI technology to find key coaching moments to help you.

- Ask your team to keep learning journals for each call.

Reflection: What are your takeaways from this section and how will you apply them to your next call review/call planning session?

Coaching territory/account review

What is the territory/account review?

The goal of the territory/accounts review is to come up with a practical strategy to maximize the yield of territory/named accounts/global accounts etc. To make this session a success, you need to get your rep to engage in strategic thinking (not just tactical thinking).

Why coach the territory review?

There are at least three good reasons why running this review will benefit your team and their results:

- It helps to eliminate a mindset of 'one-and-done', where prospecting plans are written up but never acted upon.

- It helps uncover neglected 'whitespace' where potential business opportunities are currently overlooked.

- It helps your people to come up with ideas to maximize existing relationships within accounts, and develop new ones.

Some questions to ask yourself first

- Have I trained my team in business/territory/account planning?

- How skilled are my people at mapping customers' commercial needs?

- To what extent are reps selling inside their comfort zones?

- How can I get them to expand conversations to a business level?

- How can I get them to come up with ideas before we meet?

- How can I get them to think big/think creatively/think outside the box?

- How well matched is each of my reps to their territory and accounts?

- Does each rep's plan provide a fair mix of existing and new products?

- How well are reps' plans aligned to our go-to-market strategy?

Territory review as a coaching opportunity

A coherent territory plan ensures your salespeople are focused on the opportunities that will maximize yield by allocating the appropriate territory, accounts, etc. based on their skills and experience.

You might get the ball rolling beforehand by sharing some kind of template and guidelines for submitting a formal prospecting plan for their territory/accounts.

What you are looking for from your reps is creativity and a degree of analysis.

You want to bring your reps on a journey of ambitious thinking

The coach's approach to the territory review

Average looks like this	Coaching looks like this
Approaches the review as a means to correct on small things.	Encourages strategic big-picture thinking.
Focuses on own ideas/current ideas.	Helps rep to brainstorm new ideas and harness creativity.
Approaches territory planning as an administrative task to get done.	Approaches territory planning/prospecting as a teaching opportunity.
Gets stuck into the CRM and planning without co-creation from the rep.	Gives the rep tools to help them to help themselves.
Assigns tasks to the rep without follow-up.	Holds reps accountable for action.

Preparation – things to consider before you coach territory review:

- Restate/clarify business strategic objectives and targets.

- Create a SWOT analysis (strengths, weaknesses, opportunities, threats).

- Ask salesperson/team to review existing accounts under these SWOT headings.

▷|◁

Reflection: What else do you need to gather at this stage of the review?

....

....

....

....

....

Conversation – questions you can ask in coaching the territory/account review:

- What have we not tried yet that could add more value?

- What are some of the key trends we are seeing in these industries?

- What are some of the pains we can solve but are not yet solving?

- Where are we in danger of letting the competition in the back door?

- What is the competition doing to generate new business?

- Where can you build deeper/better relationships with this client?

- Which departments/divisions can you expand your network in?

- What is your plan to get introductions to the Head of X?

- How would you rank your accounts in terms of priority?

- How realistic is your plan considering recent performance?

- What is going on with this client in other areas of the business?

- Which conversations are really going to make a difference?

- What is the minimum level of prospecting activity to win this account?

Activity: Come up with three more coaching questions you can ask here.

....

....

....

....

....

Application – next steps:

- What are your rep's agreed next steps?

- How will you keep them accountable?

- When do you expect to follow up with them?

....

....

....

....

....

....

Think like a franchisee

I like to think of salespeople as having a *franchise*. So, let's imagine that you owned the master franchise for a region or national territory as part of a fast-food chain.

You would be expected to come up with a plan to generate as much business from that area as possible. You would need to find, onboard and develop *franchisees* who could maximize revenue opportunities for you.

In that sense, the prospecting review conversation is the conversation where you might like to flip the rep from *thinking like a rep to thinking like a franchisee.*

Think like you own it

The corporation that owned all master franchises would only allocate a national franchise or regional franchise to you on the basis that you were able to co-create a plan and execute the plan and get results, right?

If you couldn't hit or exceed the targets the execs expected, you would eventually (or immediately) lose it to someone else more capable of owning that master franchise. It's as brutal as that.

Your reps are salespeople, but they are also business owners in the sense that they 'sit' on a territory and are expected to come up with a business plan to maximize its yield. Hunting for new opportunities. Farming and expanding existing ones.

Some reps might have a better feel for small to medium-sized businesses (SMB) whereas others might come up with breakthrough ideas for mid-market or Enterprise. Expect surprises.

Reflection: How can you coach your team to think of themselves like franchisees or territory-owners?

Story from practice

Khaled was preparing his first review with you. He was sitting on a healthy portfolio of accounts which he had inherited from Bob. The trouble was that Khaled wasn't expanding opportunity. He appeared to have little imagination with regards to how to *land and expand*.

You emailed Khaled with an overview of how the territory review would work and asked him to put himself in the shoes of a franchise-holder looking to get more business from his franchise.

You had given Khaled a template before the review and checked into to make sure that Bob had done a proper handover of his accounts.

You asked Khaled some simple questions to start:

- *So, what do you think you'd like to get from your territory?*

- *If you wanted another 10%, where would you start?*

- *Which are the strengths, weaknesses, opportunities and threats?*

By the end of the session, Khaled realized:

- He wasn't tapping key relationships.

- He was overlooking potential opportunities.

- He needed to better understand the business needs of key clients.

Khaled's feedback to you as his coach

I realized that I was in danger of losing out to the competition because I was not close enough to my key customers.

I'm not the best prospector in the business but I think I know how to get better and try new channels that work for me. I've got some great ideas I want to try out.

You helped me to see there was no structure or business plan to my approach. I can now see can see why everything I do must have a purpose in the larger scheme of things.

Pro tip

A SWOT analysis is a really simple coaching tool. You create four boxes labelled strengths, weaknesses, opportunities and threats.

You ask the team to review their existing accounts/territory under those four headings.

- Where are we strong, successful and difficult to displace?

- Which opportunities exist to grow revenue further?

- Where are we not selling enough?

- Where are we in danger of losing out to the competition?

- What are we missing here?

Are we thinking *big picture*? Are we thinking *big goals*? Are we thinking in terms of *revenue maximization* not just *territory management*? How are we prospecting the right accounts so we can build relationships and earn a seat at the table?

Pro tip

Imagine your team have a value proposition for business unit A. Great.

But have they overlooked value potential for business unit B? Yes? Not great.

Create a simple grid with your products down the left. Now write your customers departments / units / divisions across the top. (That's just one way).

Next, look for unexplored business opportunities in accounts and/or territory? Find any? That's your whitespace.

White-space-analysis like this helps your team to 'unlock' potential within existing accounts or territory.

And it's a great coaching exercise with teams or individuals.

- Where are we leaving money on the table?

- Where is the competition not offering value?

- How could you align with customer needs?

- What is your revenue potential here?

- What's your plan to 'landscape' the relationships?

- How can I support you to develop your plan?

So, if one thing can be achieved by coaching the territory/account review, it's getting your reps to pull their heads out of their screens. It's getting them to stop the daily sales motion of prospecting without thinking first. Step back to step up.

Closing thoughts

- How can you run the territory review in a way that creates fresh thinking?

- How would the territory review work for you as a group session?

- How could you get your reps to think ambitiously?

- How can you align the right rep with the right territory?

- How can the outputs from the session help your sales leadership?

▷|◁

Reflection: What are your takeaways from this chapter and how will you apply them to your next territory review / account planning session?

Coaching team meetings

Kevin – a recently promoted sales manager – told me: *All I ever seem to do these days since I took on this leadership position is either preparing for meetings, attending meetings, or following up on meetings. This isn't what I signed up for.*

People like Kevin are frustrated by the burden of end-to-end meetings and meetings about meetings, and meetings that don't contribute to results.

Most sales managers would rather do the kinds of things that identify, progress and close sales opportunities than clocking up *meeting miles*. True?

Meetings are often viewed as a time-suck:

- Meetings take time to prepare for.

- They cut into the productivity of the day.

- Then there's all that email/messaging back and forth afterwards.

A good number of the meetings in your calendar perhaps aren't created by you but must be attended by you: quarterly business reviews (QBRs), forecast calls, town-halls, etc.

Meetings as a coaching opportunity

But what about the ones that you schedule, organize, and run? These are the meetings that you can shape with your coaching.

If run properly, with the right people engaged, team meetings can produce highly productive opportunities to:

- Harness creativity.

- Boost productivity.

- Drive accountability.

▷|◁

Reflection: Which meetings work best for your team and why?

....

....

....

....

....

....

Every meeting is a coaching opportunity

Whether it's your regular daily stand-up, weekly or quarterly meeting, you need to leverage every team get-together as an opportunity to coach.

I have seen managers schedule 'team coaching' sessions. But you don't really need to label any team meeting as a 'coaching session'.

Coaching is how you do things. It's not what you call things

Let's look at opportunities to coach multiple people on your team all at once.

The coach's approach to the team meeting

Average looks like this	Coaching looks like this
Sets agenda.	Sets challenges.
Promotes own ideas.	Encourages input and brainstorming.
Takes on the planning.	Delegates organization to foster leadership.
Focuses on own role.	Develops team's skills and practices.
Runs the meeting as a director.	Hosts the meeting as a facilitator.

Some questions for you

- How will this meeting contribute to my success/team success?

- Does this meeting need to involve me and all/key salespeople?

- Who needs to be here and what's their contribution?

- Where is the value in delegating the chairing of the meetings to others?

- How can I turn this into an opportunity to upskill/stretch/grow?

- What can I do to motivate my team to take on new responsibility?

- What can I share with the team to change mindset/attitude?

- How can I get the team to come up with fresh ideas/new thinking?

- How can I make this meeting interactive and collaborative?

- What can I do to celebrate success and champion winning behavior?

SCRUM principles

Jeff Sutherland's book *SCRUM: The Art of Doing Twice the Work in Half the Time* changed my thinking about how I plan and run meetings.

When I qualified as a Professional Scrum Master (PSM1), it helped me to understand how software developers plan, prioritize and execute work.

There are some principles based on SCRUM which you can adapt to daily meetings (huddles/stand-ups) but equally to other meetings too.

- Same duration – *predictable time commitment*.

- Same location – *familiar environment*.

- Same time – *known schedule*.

RPI: Results, pipeline, impediments – the magic three

A powerful way to keep meetings short is to get everyone to stand up then coach on just three key things: results, pipeline, impediments.

1. Look at *results* of activity. Where are people slipping? Where are they exceeding KPIs? What are the leading indicators telling you?

   Ask: Where do you need to focus your attention right now?

2. Look at your team's *pipeline*. What needs to get done to progress key deals? Which conversations need to be executed/scheduled? What are the priorities?

   Ask: How can I help you structure your time, so you are clear and enabled for the day/week/quarter ahead?

3. Look at possible *impediments* ahead so you can remove them.

   Ask: How can I help you to uncover, understand and unblock issues before they materialize and become problems or excuses?

Coaching plan – preparation, conversation, application

Preparation – things to consider before your meetings:

- Who needs to be here and why?

- How can I get the best possible input from everyone?

- What is the opportunity to coach/challenge/stretch?

Reflection: What else do you need to look closely at and why?

Conversation – some questions you can ask your team in meetings:

- Jim, what are your top three priorities this morning?

- Shirley, what's the most important conversation for you today/this week?

- Guys, what's a better way to get an introduction to X?

- Hamid, what's your plan to set up a call with X?

- Shilpa, what could we do differently to get more traction with X?

- What's going to help us get through to more decision-makers?

- Mohammed, what's the best way to approach X?

- What's your suggestion to run this play, Kate?

Activity: Think of least three more questions and what you need to hear.

....

....

....

....

....

....

Application – some next steps to follow up:

- How will you help keep them accountable?

- How will you keep them focused on their commitments?

- How will this tie back into your reconciliation plan?

....

....

....

....

....

Pro tip

Remember that the number one goal in coaching meetings is to find ways to get your people to come away with awareness, insight and commitment.

Sure, you have administrative tasks to address but you are dealing with sales-people who need you to help them to *uncover, understand and unlock*.

Bestselling author Mike Weinberg suggests asking yourself whether your sales-people leave better equipped, aligned and energized after your meeting.

When you coach your sales team to get their involvement, input and insight, the chances are higher that they will.

Daily meetings – yes or no?

Attention, focus and energy levels are at their highest in the morning. Even if your people think they don't need coaching first thing, they often do.

Let's look at why three reasons why running a no-excuses, no-exception brief sales meeting every day could work for you.

1. **It makes punctuality an incentive.** You are conspicuous by your absence when you are not there for a meeting. It's easy to slink in and plonk down at your desk when there is nothing to be on-time for. Many remote salespeople need structure in their day.

2. **It sparks positivity in the team.** A positive action-focused, stand-up meeting first thing is a way of injecting momentum in the team. Some people clap their hands, ring a bell, high-five, others literally huddle. Whatever works. Harnessing positive energy and positive language is what coaches do on the side-lines of a game.

3. **It focuses minds on collective goals.** A well-run daily stand-up helps coach the team on what has been achieved and what has to be done. It reminds reps that they are part of a team that plays on the same side of the net. All for one and one for all.

Share the agenda

Let people know the agenda in advance. This gives them time to prepare.

For example: *Tomorrow, we are drilling into opportunities older than 125 days. Bring your oldest, best opportunity and some questions to ask yourself.*

Time is the most precious asset that you and your team have. A clear, tight agenda creates respect for time.

Put it to the floor

Use coaching to ask questions of your sales team.

Instead of saying: *Here is the way to do X,* instead say to your reps. *Here is the challenge. What is a better way to do X?*

The first approach focuses on your ideas. The second approach gets the team to come up with theirs.

As a coach, you want to get your people to co-create outcomes they can own.

Keep them on their toes

Sales meetings don't have to be boring, dry and unproductive, so shake things up a little from time to time.

Give someone a 'lightning task' to accomplish, e.g., present on a topic then get their colleagues to coach the presenter by asking three questions.

Make 'lightning' tasks easy and fun so that people improve their ability to think on their feet – just like they have to when dealing with prospects.

▷|◁

Reflection: What do you need to do today to prepare for your next productive sales meeting?

....

....

....

....

....

....

Coaching the pipeline review

Why pipeline?

I magine you are a farmer watching water flow from a pipe over the course of a year. Can you hear the sound?

For several unpredictable weeks each year, an *excess of water* pours out and you haven't enough storage or people to gather the water (too much).

The next couple of months after that, *no water* comes out and everyone is thirsty and desperate (too little).

Would you be happy living on that farm? Could you run a business like that?

What you really want is a consistent and predictable stream of supply. No floods, no droughts – just predictable amounts of water, quality of water and pressure of water when you need it.

Pipeline review as a coaching opportunity

Just as a farm needs a pipeline of water, Sales needs a pipeline or supply of deals. Without adequate *pipe*, opportunity dries up and business shrivels.

When you coach the pipeline review, you help people to see the connection between activity today and output weeks or months from now.

Stay out of the trench

You oversee the supply of qualified opportunities for your business, but your salespeople are responsible for activities that contribute to the supply.

They build those pipes, fill those pipes and maintain those pipes.

You inspect those pipes through coaching, but you do not jump into the trenches and fix those pipes. It's your salesperson's pipe.

Coaching the pipeline review

An easy place to start is to get your salesperson walking you through their 3Vs.

- Volume of pipeline – *how much is in the pipe?*

- Value of pipeline – *how much is the value of deals in the pipe?*

- Velocity of pipeline – *how quickly things are moving through the pipe?*

Going further, you can get your salesperson's thoughts on:

- Average sales cycle – *how long is the pipe?*

- Aged opportunities – *what is stuck in the pipe?*

- Coverage – *what happens if things disappear in the pipe?*

▷|◁

Reflection: Which other pipeline factors can you leverage as coaching points in your next pipeline review?

Pro tip

Try to avoid the temptation to get sucked into a specific deal.

Your goal here is to focus on the *pipeline*, not one or more deals in it. Read that again!

You can schedule a separate session for individual deals later. (See the earlier section on deal reviews.)

Pro tip

I have been told to my face by a rep that he didn't *need* to prospect because he had a never-ending supply of marketing qualified leads (MQLs).

Marketing was doing such a great job that he literally didn't have to build pipeline. He was almost outpaced by the quantity of opportunities he had.

As a coach, you want to pick up fast on any attitude where the rep thinks they don't need to prospect because *I'm good. I have enough in the pipe.*

That view is flawed. That response usually comes from those who haven't lived through a famine. All they know is a feast.

Well, actually *you're not good.*

- You are sitting on territory/accounts and that territory/accounts has/have an expected yield for which you are responsible.

- You are a sales professional, and the business pays you to prospect because it's part and parcel of your job description.

- You are a member of a sales team, and everyone has a responsibility to produce and *to be seen to produce.*

Some reps get spoiled because the pipeline is filled for them. That is until the day when the lead-machine stops working.

Those who forget to build pipeline tend to be those who crank the pump handle and watch in desperation when nothing come out.

When people depend on the business to build their pipeline, they often *unlearn* what it takes to do it themselves. Use your coaching to eliminate this mindset.

Story from practice

Greg's goal was 500K (annual contract value or ACV) and he needed 3 × coverage.

Average deal size (ADS) was 100K and you expected to see him hunt for quality opportunities with an average deal cycle (ADC) of six months.

And you also wanted to see him achieve a land vs. expand rate of approximately 50%.

This would mean that 50% of his revenue would come from new accounts and the other 50% would come from within existing accounts.

But Greg was too focused on existing business to the detriment of new business, and he couldn't see the consequences for him or the team.

Greg wasn't prospecting in Q4. *He wasn't putting anything into the pipe.*

Your concern was that he could end up in a *feast or famine* situation where he'd have nothing in the pipe for next quarter and have to scramble for new leads.

You asked Greg some helpful questions including:

- *What's your forecast looking like for Q1?*

- *How important is prospecting for new vs. progression of current ops?*

- *How much prospecting do you need to do now to come in on target?*

As Greg did the math, he realized that he was facing a dry January and possibly an even drier Q1. There was no way he would make his H1 target like that.

You listened as Greg came up with a plan to reconsider his capacity levels and his need for assistance from his peers on the complex deals he had.

Greg's feedback to you as his coach

I guess I took my foot off the gas. I forgot one of the first rules in developing a healthy sales pipeline and you reminded me of the importance of ABP [always be prospecting].

I've been too focused on two of my big deals. I should have asked for help with them so I could give more time to lining up some new calls.

I now have a clear plan to focus on rebuilding my pipe starting today including demand generation and some sales plays.

I'm also going to reach out to Liza in Sales Ops to help me line up some funnel ideas.

▷|◁

Reflection: What else would you like to hear your salesperson say?

....

....

....

....

....

Some questions to ask yourself

- Does this rep know how to present their pipeline to me?

- Have they received training on how to generate CRM reports?

- What am I going to challenge them on and congratulate them on?

- How am I comparing their pipeline to baseline (what does good look like)?

- What is the total value of their pipeline?

- What is the total volume of their pipeline?

- What is the 'capacity'/'ability' of this rep to close larger deals?

- What is the average sales cycle length?

- Where are some deals possibly stagnating?

- What is the coverage against quota this rep needs in this quarter?

- Which opportunities are closing simultaneously?

- Are there deals which are being pushed out repeatedly or converging?

- Are there deals which have an unusually short sales cycle?

- What is the 'mix' of opportunities to have a healthy pipe for this rep?

Preparation – things to consider before you coach the pipeline review:

- *What are the possible risks in your salesperson's pipeline?*

- *How happy are you with their win rates, activity, etc.?*

- *What do you need to address e.g., ADS, capacity, qualification?*

▷|◁

Reflection: What else do you need to look closely at and why?

....

....

....

....

....

....

Conversation – some questions you can ask your rep in coaching:

- How is your pipeline going to help you achieve x personal goal?

- On a scale of one to five, how would you rate the integrity of your pipeline?

- Where are the bottlenecks/risks in your pipeline right now?

- Where do you foresee problems one/three/six months from now?

- What can you do now to progress opportunities faster? (Velocity question.)

- What can you do to improve the quality of opportunities? (Value question.)

- What can you do to get more into your pipeline? (Volume question.)

- Where do you need help to up your prospecting activity?

- What's your plan to clean out the stagnant/zombie deals from the pipe?

- How confident are you that your pipeline is going to produce results?

Activity: Think of least three more questions and what you need to hear.

....

....

....

....

....

....

Actions – some next steps to follow up:

- When is your next scheduled check-in lined up?
- How will you keep them focused on their commitments?
- How will this tie back into your reconciliation plan?

....

....

....

....

....

The coach's approach to the pipeline review

Average looks like this	Coaching looks like this
Focuses on numbers only.	Focuses on the salesperson's success.
Moves deals without consultation.	Enlists the salesperson's thinking to manage capacity.
Decides actions and priorities.	Involves the salesperson in coming up with a plan.
Dives straight into solutions.	Shares stories from own experience of managing pipeline.
Tries the same approach to pipeline generation.	Facilitates the creation of a motivating pipeline generation plan with buy-in.

▷|◁

Reflection: What are your takeaways from this chapter and how will you apply them to your next territory review/account planning session?

....

....

....

....

....

Coaching the performance review

What is the performance review?

The performance review is usually a private conversation that takes place to cover a range of things not addressed by some of the other reviews in this book.

The performance review addresses the totality of your salesperson's performance for that given period.

Not just metric-driven aspects related to sales but also relationship aspects such as attitude, co-operation, resilience, mindset, etc.

Why it matters

Top sales leaders view the performance review as a two-way street. It's a chance to coach and it's a great opportunity to get feedback on your leadership.

The main purpose is to review your rep's results. A secondary purpose is to provide some developmental coaching.

The outcome of a proper performance review is a jointly developed plan for individual improvement. Achieving this requires input from both parties.

Why it sometimes doesn't go to plan

The key thing to keep in mind is that you are there to review *performance*, not the *person*. It's a subtle but important difference.

I have seen managers appraise the results of someone on their team, but they do in such a way that the rep feels *they* are being reviewed rather than performance.

The consequence? Defensiveness, resistance and sometimes hostility.

3 reasons the review can be problematic

1. The performance review is often perceived to be corrective by design. Your rep may clam up and the coaching dialogue becomes an appraisal monologue.

2. Most performance conversations are entirely retrospective in nature (backwards-looking), whereas they should also be perspective (forward-looking).

3. Many leaders don't get training to run performance reviews. Winging it has implications for your reps' compensation, career-success and self-confidence.

It takes courage to coach performance

We'd all rather avoid reviewing performance if we've not yet learned to be comfortable doing it, or when we find ourselves coaching difficult people.

Reviewing performance is an act of courage and it's something you can't outsource to someone else simply because you don't feel comfortable doing it.

Pro tip

The performance review demands preparation so you can address specific instances where things like co-operation and attitude are a problem.

When you are doing all the talking, your performance review will be brief and to the point. But that's not co-creative and it's not effective either.

Just as in other reviews covered in this book, you need a healthy balance of listening and talking. Anywhere from 30 to 60 minutes should suffice.

The performance review as a coaching opportunity

Your salesperson is walking you through things like:

- How they make decisions.

- How they manage their time.

- How they are developing their skillset.

- How they are tracking to their personal goals.

- How they see themselves evolving under your leadership.

You are listening actively for opportunities to:

- Get feedback.

- Share useful stories.

- Praise and encourage.

- Provide some mentoring.

- Develop trust and openness.

The performance review is an excellent opportunity to use the 3-U™ coaching model explained at the beginning of this book

- Uncover – *What's holding you back?*

- Understand – *What exactly is the challenge?*

- Unlock – *What can be done to solve it?*

Work with your rep to *uncover* issues, *understand* blockages and *unlock* ways forward. Coaching at this level can be personally very rewarding.

Find one specific thing that you can genuinely praise, however small, e.g. *I like the way you are taking your time to do X well.*

Some questions to ask yourself before you coach

- Have I a good sense of where this rep is performing/underperforming?
- Have they a clear understanding of excellent/satisfactory/underperforming?
- Have I given frequent interim feedback, so they can improve?
- Has the salesperson been given time to prepare their own review?
- Have I given them an agenda of the areas/cases the review will focus on?
- Have I set aside enough time to give them a fair and adequate hearing?
- Is their performance indicative of how well I have led them?
- What is the root cause of this behavior?
- Is this an issue which has the potential to cause toxicity in the team?
- Is this salesperson facing challenges that I cannot help with?
- Is this a matter that coaching can address or is this person on the way out?
- How can I leverage our time together to help change perspective?

Pro tip

You can address an aspect of performance while the rep is still focused on the task rather than waiting until *after the fact*.

Feedback is information and it has a *best-before date* so give your salespeople performance feedback in real-time where possible.

Story from practice

Stephanie was dreading the performance review. In her last place of work, she usually felt *ambushed*.

She never knew what was on the agenda. Performance criteria appeared to be arbitrary. She didn't think it was either fair or objective.

Her last manager usually took out his notes of all the times that she had missed targets and made mistakes. But you did things differently.

- You explained the format in advance.

- You outlined what would be covered.

- You highlighted what was being measured.

- You showed her how the review would help her.

You put some careful thought into what you could highlight both as developmental feedback as well as evaluative feedback.

You put Stephanie at ease and made her feel like a valued member of the team. There were some areas for improvement, but you handled them well.

You learned something that you could not have known unless Stephanie confided in you. Now a couple of things were making a lot more sense.

The more you talked and exchanged ideas, the more you understood what motivated Stephanie and how you could do a better job of supporting her.

- She learned to see you as a mentor and a coach.

- Stephanie came away with some valuable feedback.

- Stephanie had new ideas on how to improve performance.

Stephanie's feedback to you as her coach

I have a better handle on how I am perceived by you and others in the team.

I am going to focus on one key area this month — improving how I manage my time.

There was a fair balance between things I am doing well and where I need to improve.

Most of all, thank you for listening to me with empathy. It's been a really difficult year for personal reasons. Thanks for your support.

Pro tip

The better managers see performance reviews as a two-way street. On the one hand, they have specific feedback which they want to share with the rep.

On the other hand, they want to solicit feedback from the rep as part of a *how am I doing as your leader?* conversation.

Your rep is far more likely to be open to insight from you if you are open to insight from them. Makes sense?

No one has any business coaching others unless they too are *coachable*. Read this again.

Being 'coachable' means that you always are open to feedback and insight from leadership, peers and/or direct reports.

When you demonstrate that you are learning and willing to learn from others, it stands to reason others will be willing to learn from you.

Coaches go first.

Coaching plan - preparation, conversation, application

Preparation – some things to consider before you coach:

- What were the agreed goals for this period?

- Which performance issues need to be addressed?

- What would I like to see them start doing/keep doing/stop doing?

Reflection: What else do you need to consider so you can open this performance conversation on the right note?

....

....

....

....

....

Conversation – some questions you can ask in coaching:

- Describe to me how this quarter has gone?

- How can I create better conditions for you to succeed?

- What have been some of the highlights of this past quarter?

- How will you rate your performance against that of your team?

- Which relationships would you most like to develop?

- What will it take to overcome your current challenge(s)?

- What do you feel is holding you back the most?

- What would you do differently if you had the power?

- Which area/skill do you want to improve this quarter?

- What is the effect of your performance on your team?

- Which of these goals are you going to prioritize and why?

Reflection: What else could you ask to make this a powerful conversation?

....

....

....

....

....

....

Application – next steps:

- What has your salesperson called out as areas for development?
- How can you help them to improve performance?
- How will I keep them accountable?

....

....

....

....

....

....

The coach's approach to the performance review

Average looks like this	Coaching looks like this
Uses the review as an opportunity to criticize.	Treats the review as a chance to learn for both parties.
Focuses on corrective feedback.	Focuses on both evaluative and developmental feedback.
Addresses past performance only.	Sets the salesperson up for future performance.
Creates a mechanical, impersonal atmosphere.	Shows genuine empathy.
Doesn't gain commitment post-review.	Seeks commitment to improve.

Pro tip

Split the performance review into two parts: *evaluative* and *developmental*.

In the evaluative part, you are reviewing together aspects of your rep's recent performance.

You are then benchmarking it against expected levels of performance *and* agreed levels of improvement since the last performance review.

In the developmental part, you are coaching on the things that will develop and lock-in future performance.

Pro tip

Resist the temptation to coach on a load of separate items in the performance review. It's inefficient in so far as you will realistically not cover all items.

You may start things that cannot be finished. You may also get stuck on something incidental rather than coaching the main item to be covered.

Focus: Follow one conversation until success

. . . .

Part 3

Coaching reactively

Using coaching when things go wrong

Using the 3-U™ model, you can help your reps to get unstuck by thinking for themselves and coming up with a series of actions.

You want top sales performers who are autonomous. This means coaching them to:

- Think for themselves.
- Regulate themselves.
- Correct themselves.
- Develop themselves.
- Lead themselves.

Sounds impossible. But it's not. It starts with you and the self-leadership you are creating through your coaching.

So in this part of your book, we're going to look at how you can use your coaching skills when things don't go to plan.

Not asking for help

Whether C-suite, managers or front-line reps, everyone needs help. In her book, *Reinforcements: How to Get People to Help You*, author Heidi Grant Halvorson suggests that we all need the collaboration and support of others. Without such help, we can't win.

Think about it. As a sales leader, you are in the business of selling help and your customers aren't too proud to ask for that help. That's why they buy it from you in the form of products and service.

Sales is simply the provision of such help at a profit. Do you agree? Your role here is to coach your people to ask for help when they need it and to get them to think how they can coach others who need help too.

#help!

When you began your sales career, you didn't know very much initially, right? You had to fill in information gaps. You had to talk to people to get a feel for things. You had to put your hand up.

You had to be willing to say that you didn't know something or didn't understand something or had forgotten something. If you didn't, you struggled unnecessarily.

No lone wolves, please

And that's the point: *unnecessarily*. Hopefully you didn't think like a *MacGyver* or a *Bear Grylls* who likes to figure everything out on their own.

You need people who work *within* your team, *as part of* your team and *for* your team.

That means hiring people who work interdependently. Not *independently* (whether high-performing or not).

▷|◁

Reflection: Think of a time when you perhaps did not ask for help. What were the consequences and where could you have benefited from getting someone to give you some perspective?

....

....

....

....

....

....

You need your people to be able to put up their hands and admit that they need your guidance, help, insight, support, etc.

To achieve this, you need to quash any stigma about asking for help. How do you do this? You make sure your team see you asking for help.

My old boss Ben used to take the opportunity *to be seen* to ask for help by his team. *Hey, guys! I've been working on X over the weekend and have to admit that I'm struggling a little. Who can give me 15 mins of their downtime before Wednesday? I need help specifically with X.*

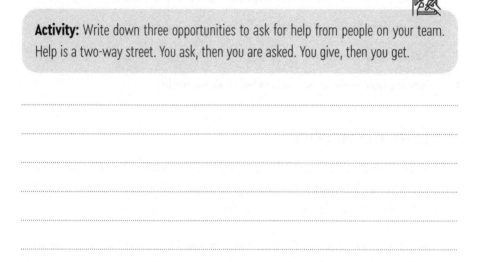

Activity: Write down three opportunities to ask for help from people on your team. Help is a two-way street. You ask, then you are asked. You give, then you get.

....

....

....

....

....

....

Why not asking for help is a problem for you

So, what's the consequence if your people are not asking for help? Ryan McNitzky, a Regional Account Director, suggests that it bugs him when salespeople don't reach out to him or colleagues to ask for help.

When you have people who appear to feel that asking for help is demeaning:

- They are more likely to struggle unnecessarily.

- They are more likely to bring issues to you late in the game.

- They are more likely to waste opportunities and precious time.

- They are less likely to help others in your sales organization.

- They are less likely to be open and frank.

- They are less likely to be successful as salespeople.

Top-down vulnerability

Ben's demonstration of vulnerability is a prime leadership quality which two London Business School professors, Rob Goffee and Gareth Jones refer to in their book *Why Should Anyone Be Led by You?*

Followers are more comfortable when their leader has shown that they are less than perfect. There is of course a difference between asking *occasionally* and *constantly*. That sends out the wrong signals.

Reflection: Which areas do you not want to ask for help as a leader and why?

It's against their nature

Your sales people naturally think of themselves as problem solvers. It's in their DNA. They want to demonstrate competence and confidence both internally and externally.

So, it goes against the grain of that perception if they need to ask for help. I want your people to ask you for help when needed but to also come to the table with possible solutions.

Activity: Write down three possible reasons why your salespeople are not asking for help.

....

....

....

....

....

....

I want your people to ask you for help when needed but to also come to the table with possible solutions

. . . .

The value of self-help

This is exactly where coaching facilitates *self-help*. They *have* a problem. They *own* the problem.

They need you to help them to figure out their possible options to solve their problem.

Coaching allows you to solve the problem *with them* without taking over the process of solving the problem *for* them.

Coaching allows you to solve the problem with them without taking over the process of solving the problem for them

Feeling good about asking

When I run deal reviews with AEs, they are primed to seek the help they get and to appreciate it.

They are hungry for it because it's going to help them get their deal over the line.

Coaching helps your people to ask for help in a way that they feel good about it and learn from it.

Trouble starts when people really need help but don't or won't ask for it.

Baart's view

Baart, a Dutch Sales Engineer told me that more often than he cares to remember, he has been brought in too late to help with an opportunity:

I can help [salespeople] understand their customers and build a water-tight technical case. But they don't ask soon enough, and we lose important deals.

I can't make miracles. I just wish they'd bring me into the conversation earlier so I can help them. That's what I'm here for.

Not asking costs people, money, sales

There is no excuse not to avail of the collective wisdom in the sales organization especially when there are people qualified, willing and available to help.

Salespeople not asking for help is a chronic problem. It's costing you time. It's costing the business revenue. It's costing people their jobs.

It's in your interest to hire people who ask for help early, quickly and often so they can get unstuck fast. At the core of getting unstuck is the ability to recognize when you can't do it on your own (#help).

Activity: Write down a story you can tell your team that highlights how you have asked for help in the past and how you/the team/the client benefited because of getting help. Now practice telling this story, so it feels natural and comfortable.

- What was the challenge/situation?
- What did you do to ask for help?
- What was the outcome?

....

....

....

....

....

Some questions to ask yourself

- What am I doing to encourage authentic vulnerability?

- How often do I ask for help from my direct reports (DRs)/leaders?

- What have I done lately to create buddies and mentor relationships?

- Have I made it clear where I expect people to ask for help?

- Am I doing anything to propagate the disease of perfectionism?

- How do I react when people ask me for help?

- How often do I remember to say 'thank you' for offers of help?

- How do I highlight people who ask for help, e.g., on Slack or meetings?

- Where in the sales process are my people not asking for help?

- Where are individual contributors/my team getting stuck?

- Where are there instances of my team not asking for help from others?

- What is telling me this person is too proud to ask for help?

- What is the best way to tactfully offer help when it's unsolicited?

- How can I begin a 'help' conversation with this specific person?

▷◁

Reflection: Ask yourself how you communicate your beliefs about asking for help. Have you unconsciously created this behavior through your own action or inaction? When? Why?

Setting the scene for coaching Lidia

In this coaching conversation, you are checking in with Lidia who is a recent addition to your team. She is struggling in several respects and appears reluctant to ask for help from her colleagues.

At team meetings, she rarely voices an opinion and never asks questions. She prefers to find her own answers to her own challenges.

The trouble is that this approach is not working. Lidia is unaware that her *allergy to asking for help* is damaging her performance, her pipeline, and her prospects (career).

You don't want lone wolves. You want team players so you decide to set aside time to reshape Lidia's perception of her role and yours.

Coaching plan - preparation, conversation, application

Preparation – some things to consider before you coach Lidia:

- Have I made it clear where I expect everyone to ask for help?

- Where is Lidia not reaching out to me and her colleagues?

- What is the quality of my relationship with Lidia?

▷|◁

Reflection: What else will set you up for this conversation?

Conversation – questions you can ask your rep in coaching:

- How are things going? (World's simplest question.)
- Where do you think you could benefit from listening to others?
- Where can you help newer members of the team?
- If I were in your shoes, where would I ask for advice right now?
- What can I do to make X easier/clearer/quicker for you?
- Where can I help you to prospect/negotiate/close better?
- Where are you finding things difficult/draining/demanding?
- Where would sharing your burden make life easier for you?
- What's the one thing I can help you to take off your plate?
- Where can getting unstuck help you right this minute?
- Where can you help the other guys on the team?

Activity: Come up with three more coaching questions you can ask here.

....

....

....

....

....

Application – next steps:

- Which actions has Lidia agreed to take on?

- How will you keep Lidia accountable for this activity?

- When will you follow up with her next?

....

....

....

....

....

....

Some tips to prepare for this coaching conversation

1. Prepare a story that highlights a time you were in Lidia's shoes and chose not to ask for help.

2. Research a specific example of how Lidia's current lone wolf behavior is costing her personally.

3. Consider which knowledge and skills Lidia can draw on to help others in her team.

4. Think of ways to get Lidia to realize that her interest is best served by seeking help.

5. Draw up a list of the ways that the go-to-market organization can actually help her. She may not know.

Excerpt from sample coaching conversation

Conversation	Coaching analysis
You: Hey, Lidia! What's going on?	*Simple, open conversation-starter*
Lidia: Hi, I'm fine.	*A little defensive. Sounds like Lidia has her guard up.*
You: So, thanks for your time. Do you remember the *Loom* I sent you last week?	*You sent Lidia a personalized video highlighting the three main qualities you expect to see in her first 100 days.*
Lidia: Sure. I watched it. Thanks.	
You: I had fun making that because it reminded me of what has made our team (and our business) great. We have built a great brand helping our customers. That has meant hiring people who want to help and ask for help. It's a two-way street. Was that message clear from the video?	*You recap the message that is most relevant to this conversation: You want your people to offer help and to seek help. You ask a straight question to check that this is understood.*
Lidia: Yeah. It was.	*Lidia confirms it's understood.*
You: Cool. You know, I've listened to several of your calls, and you are doing an excellent job of discovery conversations. I'm curious: Where did you learn that?	*You have planned this conversation so that you can invite Lidia to offer her help using one of her strengths.*
Lidia: I got some great training over at X when I joined, and my mentor Matt was amazing. He helped me with discovery calls.	*Lisa highlights how she benefited from help in her previous role.*
You: So, Matt helped you with discovery calls?	*You repeat Lidia's words exactly as you heard them.*
Lidia: He did. A lot.	
You: Right. Did you ask for that help, or did he offer?	*You clarify what instigated the help.*

Conversation	Coaching analysis
Lidia: It was part of the training. The next time, he offered, and the next time after that I came to him for guidance.	*Lidia confirms that help was sought and offered. This is exactly what you want to hear.*
You: What made you ask for his guidance?	*You want Lidia to clarify her motivation.*
Lidia: I had no choice because I had tried everything myself.	*Lidia indicates that she does not have all the answers.*
You: Really? So what happened next?	*You keep Lidia talking to get more of the picture.*
Lidia: Do you mean with the opportunity? I lost it.	*Bingo.*
You: Got it. [Pause]	*You let it hang…1, 2, 3…*
You: So, I have a favor to ask. I'd like Saaqib to ask for help. He's trying to do everything himself even when he can't and that's a big problem around here. If there is one thing I look for in my team, it's willingness to give help and ask for help. Do you think you can help with that like Matt helped you?	*You pivot here to get Lidia in a position where she wants to help someone on your team who needs her help. This sets a behavioral precedent and makes it easier to get her to ask for help where she needs it most.*
Lidia: I think so. What do you need?	*Lidia is on board.*
You: So together you and I need to think of an approach that will make it clear to Saaqib that he needs guidance with making better discovery calls. How do you think I can get that message across? I need your help with that.	*You phrase this request in such a way that it sounds like Saaqib needs help. He does. But subconsciously, Lidia realizes that people like her need to be open to help. You invite Lidia to make suggestions to help people with this mindset. You ask for her help.*
Lidia: Sure. Umm… Could I ask him if he just needs help with his discovery calls?	*Suggestion 1.*

Conversation	Coaching analysis
You: OK. What else?	*You ask Lidia for more ideas.*
Lidia: I could create a resource that helps Saaqib and walk him through it.	*Suggestion 2.*
You: Sure. What else?	*You ask Lidia again for more ideas.*
Lidia: I could think of an example when I asked Matt for help over at X and I improved.	*Suggestion 3.*
You: OK. Those are great suggestions, Lidia. Which one(s) most makes sense to you given your current priorities?	*You make it clear that you appreciate Lidia's creative process and ask her to select an option she has suggested.*
Lidia: I think I can share some of my examples with him and offer to help with one of his opportunities.	*Lidia exercises her judgment.*
You: OK. How can I help you with that?	*You test whether Lidia has gotten the message and is open to help.*
Lidia: Can you make an introduction to Saaqib. I haven't actually had a convo with him yet.	*She makes her first request for help. Great work.*
You: No problem. I'll do that for you.	*You agree to help her.*
You: I really appreciate your help, Lidia. And I'm sure that Saaqib's going to really appreciate it to. I want to pay this forward, so the final step is to see where I can help you.	*You thank Lidia and confirm the benefit of helping another team member. You can now ask Lidia directly to indicate where she needs help.*
Lidia: Uh. OK. Makes sense.	
You: When you interviewed for your first team last year, I note that you said you really want to be a manager. It's really important that our managers see themselves as servant-leaders first.	*For the purpose of reinforcement, you link the new behavior you wish to see with Lidia's own self-interest.*

Conversation	Coaching analysis
You: Where can I and the team help you to achieve your target, so you are in the best possible position to be eligible for that career track?	*You invite Lidia to ask for help where she really needs it. Lidia's got the message.*

Closing questions for you

- How can I make a point of rewarding someone who asks for help?

- What do forecasts tell me about my teams' thinking, not just their selling?

- What does the quality of my forecasts say about my sales leadership?

In this chapter, you learned that everyone needs help. That's why it's extremely important to hire people who are OK with helping as well as being helped. You also learned that help starts with you.

When you ask for help, you make it clear that you don't have all the answers. No one does.

When you encourage your team to help others on their team, you open their minds to being helped too.

But there is a fine line between asking for help occasionally and asking for help consistently. Coaching your salespeople works when they are willing to help themselves first.

Coaching allows you to solve the problem with them without taking over the process of solving the problem *for* them.

Not using the CRM

All that data that you have in your CRM right now as you read this is a valuable capital asset. Many organizations don't reflect it on their balance sheets, but they should. It's all those client names. It's the record of all those conversations and touch points.

It's all the commercial intelligence gathered by your reps concerning decision-makers, decision processes and criteria, business needs and company structure, all distilled into a database.

It's all the value captured thanks to thousands (or millions) of hours prospecting in the marketplace. How much is it worth to you?

Reflection: Ask yourself how happy you are with quality of content in your CRM and the consistency with which your reps update it.

- What is the value of all the information you are collecting but not capturing?

- What is the value of all the information you should have?

- Why are we not putting it in the system?

It's not as if you aren't paying a substantial amount for your CRM.

It's not as if you can do without the software which runs all your campaigns and enables you to create valuable dashboards.

It's not as if your team haven't been *trained* on how to use Salesforce, Dynamics, Pipedrive, Close, etc. So, what's stopping them?

That's the most important question to figure. You can then use coaching to create behavioral change.

▷|◁

Reflection: Who needs to be coached by you on using your CRM properly and why?

....

....

....

....

....

....

It's a must not an ask

The answer is they are not being coached to do it. It's not being driven (again and again) that they absolutely must. It's what your team are paid to do.

From my perspective, updating the CRM with the most important information gathered each day is *non-negotiable*.

It's an integral part of being a sales professional. It's not an ask. It's a must.

Your CRM is gold-dust. It's all those client names. It's the record of all those conversations and touch points

Why not updating the CRM is a problem for you

CRM adoption (or the lack of it) is an expensive problem.

Many sales managers are invariably unhappy with reps forgetting to (or deciding not to) update the CRM. Is this true for you too?

- Perhaps your CRM is cumbersome (technical issue).

- Perhaps reps can't navigate the system (knowledge issue).

- Maybe they just don't bother (attitude issue).

- Or they are not being coached for reinforcement (behavioral issue).

So which is it?

Activity: Write down three possible reasons why your salespeople are not using and updating prospect data in your CRM on a regular basis.

Reflection: What is the cost to you if your team don't? What evidence do you have? What are you going to do about it?

....

....

....

....

....

....

Some questions to ask yourself

- When did my guys last receive any training on the CRM?

- Who delivered the training and what was the format?

- Have they been certified on how to use the CRM?

- Which aspects of the CRM (if any) are slowing my reps down?

- When did I last try using the CRM exactly as one of my reps has to?

- Which reports could I run to find out how the CRM is being used?

- How would it help if I build a report showing the cost of the CRM to the business?

- Which reports would show a picture of overall usage of the CRM?

- What kind of incentivization would work to change behavior?

- How can I use consequence coaching to enforce behavioral change?

- How could I enlist the support of senior leadership to drive CRM adoption?

- Have I already addressed this topic with this rep/the team?

- Which kinds of coaching conversations do I need to have?

- Who is the first person I need to have a conversation with?

- How will I prepare for this conversation with them?

- How could I enlist marketing to create an internal CRM adoption campaign?

- What kinds of resources (e.g., videos) would help the team?

▷|◁

Reflection: What kind of new behavior do you want to see in place around CRM usage?

....

....

....

....

....

....

Some coaching questions to ask your rep(s)

- *How good would you say is your knowledge of the CRM?*

- *What do you think is the value of the data in the CRM?*

- *What do you do with all the information I hear you gathering?*

- *When you go to meet a prospect what happens to all your notes?*

- *What can I/Sales Ops/Enablement do to help you use the CRM?*

- *What can you do to remind yourself of the importance of updating records?*

- *What is your plan to clean up the 'zombies' (dead records)?*

- *What is your process for adding call details to the CRM?*

- *What's your rationale for doing things this way?*

- *What is the quality of the information in CRM worth to you right now?*

- *How would having better data help you to land bigger deals?*

- *What's it going to take so we don't have to have this conversation again?*

Activity: Come up with at least three more coaching questions you can ask your team to help them understand the critical importance of updating the CRM.

....

....

....

....

....

....

Some tips to prepare for this coaching conversation

- Gather stats from Sales Ops that show how this rep is using the CRM.

- Dig into a sample of their records to pull out great examples/poor examples.

- Consider the technical knowledge proficiency/training records of your rep.

- Check whether you have raised this topic in a previous coaching conversation.

- Check your rep's calendar for a suitable time to coach.

- Create a clear goal so you can be sure that your conversation has a purpose.

- Come up with a way to open the conversation.

- Clarify the outcome/agreement you want from your rep(s).

- Consider whether to run this as a one-to-one or as a group session to save time.

Setting the scene for coaching Jim on using the CRM

In this sample conversation, your coaching records show that you have already had a conversation with Jim about this issue.

You want to reveal that Lisa – one of your directors – is taking a keen interest in driving/enforcing CRM adoption.

Your goal here is to highlight the cost to the business *and to Jim* of not having reliable data for prospecting.

You decide to enlist Jim's help to get the team to use it.

Excerpt from sample coaching conversation

Conversation	Coaching analysis
You: Hey Jim. Thanks for your time today.	*Thank Jim for taking time from his schedule to meet.*
You: How is it going with the Mid-Market campaign?	*Wait for the answer.*
Jim: Pretty good.	
You: That's good to hear. In fact, I can see that you are doing *pretty good* on the leader board. You're in fourth position this week. Is that right?	*Confirming you are aware of how Jim is doing and setting yourself up to pay a specific compliment then asking an easy question for Jim to answer.*
Jim: Yeah. I'm trying hard on this one. I expect to hit goal with a bit more luck. It's a lot better than last month. Yep.	*Jim acknowledges the compliment.*
You: Nice work. You're saying that *it's a lot better than last month.* So what's making the difference this for you this time?	*Complimenting Jim further and repeating his words to allow you to dig for an answer to your next question.*
Jim: So, the quality of the leads coming in from marketing is good, actually. OK... a lot better this time. At least better than last month.	*Jim answers confirming that the quality of the information in the leads is good.*
You: So, when you say that the *quality of the leads coming in is a lot better than last month* – what's making them better?	*You paraphrase Jim's response and use it as a bridge to ask a clarification question.*
Jim: I don't know but we've got more to go on. You know. I've got telephone numbers I can call. The email addresses haven't been scraped from who-knows-where this time. They're good too.	*Jim expands on his answer, giving you ideas to agree with him and use this to illustrate the value of data integrity in the CRM.*

Conversation	Coaching analysis
You: I get it. So, you've got *telephone numbers you can call* and the email addresses are *good*. Yeah, I can imagine that makes a difference! [Laughs]	*You understand and repeat his words for confirmation.*
Jim: Yeah. [Laughs]	*You share a story that illustrates you know what it's like to be in his position/role. This builds empathy.*
You: I can remember what it was like, I had to call the switchboard and charm someone to put me through. I would have killed for those numbers.	*You replay Jim's words so you can prepare to challenge the current usage of the CRM. You ask him to create an image in his mind of a situation where he would be in a position which he has confirmed he does not want to be in.*
Jim: You had no numbers? At all?	*Jim confirms the value of having data integrity in the CRM and the cost to him of having data issues.*
You: OK. We had some but we didn't have a subscription to [service name]. And that was before we had marketing pump out MQLs. Back up. A moment ago, you said that *quality of the leads coming from marketing is good*. So, what do you think is the impact of having those numbers to call? I mean, *imagine* I just gave you the company name but no number in our CRM. What would you do?	*You inform Jim of the effort and value of what goes into the CRM and remind him (using his words) of what it would be like to have no valid data to call on.*
Jim: [Pause] Mmmm. I'd just have to call and take my chances, I guess. But that would suck.	*Jim acknowledges your point.*

Conversation	Coaching analysis
You: OK. So, bear with me. We have to pay for that information from [service name]. That goes into our CRM. Next, marketing does a great job creating landing pages using [service name] and all that goes into the CRM. It's not perfect. But it's better than having no number to call. You said *that would suck*.	*You stress the critical nature of having a CRM as a sales intelligence system (SIS) that Jim can rely on.*
Jim: [Pause] OK. Yeah. It would.	
You: So, to me, the CRM makes us or breaks us. Know what I mean?	*You decide to check whether Jim has any solid reason why he is not using your CRM.*
Jim: True. Yeah. I guess.	*Jim confirms that there is (in this instance) no real issue preventing him from using the CRM.*
You: Just so I'm clear, is there anything that could be stopping you from using the CRM?	*Because you know that Jim has already been approached about this in a previous conversation, you are now making it crystal clear that there are no more excuses. You are not beating around the bush on this one. You also remind me him that this is not a big ask.*
Jim: Well. I get slammed now and again and I kinda just forget.	*Jim is a little monosyllabic because he knows that there is no place to hide.*
You: So, here's the thing. We're paying megabucks for our CRM. It's mandated that we use it to gather every sales conversation and touchpoint. I ran a report today and it's not good. I really need to see you guys filling in these fields and completing these dropdowns. I mean that takes all of 60 seconds, right?	*You ask Jim for his help (compliance). You remind Jim that senior leadership is aware of the situation.*

Conversation	Coaching analysis
Jim: Yeah. Maybe.	*You invite Jim to co-create ideas that he will 'own' and that these can be shared with leadership directly with his name on them if you decide.*
You: I need your *help* because CRM adoption is not where it is and Lisa [Director] is not happy with it. Let's get some ideas on to *Mural* or we can whiteboard it right now. Alright with you? As we come up with good ideas, we can share these with Lisa. Cool? So let's start with this. What can we do to get more guys like you to update it so you and the team don't have to call and *take your chances*?	*You ask Jim to get involved in coming up with workable suggestions. You play his words back to him for effect.*
Jim: What about…	*Jim goes first.*

Closing thoughts

- Could you find out whether your reps have been given standardized training to use your CRM?

- Could you enlist help from Sales Ops to establish whether there are challenges with the way that your CRM is set up?

- Could you instigate a campaign to get your reps to *tombstone* old records so that your CRM doesn't become a ZRM (zombie record management) system?

Not organizing themselves

There is a powerful self-coaching question I came across several years ago. I love it and it's important to ask it of yourself every single day:
What would my team be… if everyone in it was just like me?

It really makes you think, doesn't it? Your team's level of self-organization and performance is a reflection of you.

How organized are you?

It's a slightly uncomfortable reality-check when you realize that your team encapsulates all the behaviors of your leadership style:

- Those that you embody.

- Those you pay attention to.

- Those you choose to ignore.

And don't think that your senior leadership don't notice.

If you want to see your people take personal responsibility or adopt any kind of positive behavior, you first have to look in the mirror.

What would the world be... if everyone in it was just like me?

....

▷|◁

Reflection: What does your team's level of self-organization say about your brand of self-leadership?

Organized people are easier to coach

As I alluded to in Part 1 of this book, recruiting the right people with a proven track-record of managing *themselves* (not just managing territory) is key. Not just for the business, but for you.

When you've got people who are accountable and self-directing, it's going to free you up to focus on a range of priorities which demand your attention as sales leader.

Dan Skipp, EMEA SDR Manager at Sophos told me:

> The biggest single contributor to my success as a sales manager is my people's capability. I need to be able to delegate certain things so I can spend more time deskside coaching.

Dan has hit the nail on the head. You need time to focus on those things that move the needle. You can't do that if you have people who can't move their own needle, right?

This means that you must be organized before you can possibly help or motivate others on your team to be organized.

Activity: Write down three possible reasons why your salespeople are not organizing themselves. What's the cost to you of having to chase people? What evidence do you have? What are you going to do about it?

....

....

....

....

Self-discipline is the hard bit

During a seven-module sales management program I was leading for a UK SaaS business, we were doing an opportunity walk-through using MEDDIC. Then we discovered that there were gaps throughout.

Kevin, the new manager, sighed and said sheepishly that he would get the missing information in Salesforce filled in. He even apologized to me.

I realized that there was an important point to be made so I asked him:

> *Hey, Kevin Remind me: Whose opportunity is this?*
>
> Rob's.
>
> *Right. So who's going to get the info? You or Rob?*
>
> Rob.
>
> *Right.*

This is his opportunity. If you do Rob's job, who's going to do yours? That was your old job, right?

Kevin needs Rob to be self-disciplined so Kevin doesn't end up shouldering the burden.

Selling is the easy bit

When I spoke with Caroline McCrystal, recipient of the Most Distinguished Saleswoman of the Year Award 2019, she said that winning her award was a result of the discipline and self-reliance that she learned when training as an elite track athlete.

When she learned to sell, she already had the self-discipline to consistently do the things that would enable her to hit target. Selling was the easy bit.

Think of it like this: every waking moment, you have four choices: *do*, *delay*, *delete* and *delegate*. It's the same set of choices your sales reps have.

If you are not *delegating* the basics like self-management to your reps, you end up *delaying* your job and you possibly end up *doing* their job. Is that true for you?

Everyone needs a daily system

Here's what Julie, a Director of Sales in Dallas-Fort Worth, told me she tells her ambitious sales leaders:

- You do *your* job.

- You hire people who can do *their* job.

- You find time to prepare for your *next* job.

To achieve this as a sales leader, you need is to ensure that each member of your sales team has their own daily system in place.

- It doesn't have to be yours.

- It doesn't have to be perfect.

- It doesn't have to mirror someone else's.

- It just needs to be a system that works for that person and your team.

If your team can't do their job, you're going to have a hard time doing yours.

▷|◁

Reflection: Who needs to be coached by you, so they can become better organized?

....

....

....

....

....

Some questions to ask yourself

- Which behaviors confirm to me that my team are responsible and self-directing?

- What is the cost to the business, to me and to my rep if they are not organized?

- Has the team received time management training?

- How can I facilitate it, so the team figure out their daily/weekly priorities?

- Where will getting the team to organize themselves pay the greatest dividends?

- How is my example influencing the team?

- What does a well-structured day/week look like?

- Which of my asks are taking my team away from their priorities?

- How would instigating prospecting blocks/call blocks/meeting blocks help?

- What tells me that the team need to be better organized?

- How could color-coding time blocks help the visual people on my team?

- How could I do a better job of hiring people who are highly organized?

- Who can I enlist to help drive self-organization as part of our sales culture?

- Which rituals/routines/rewards will help to champion personal organization?

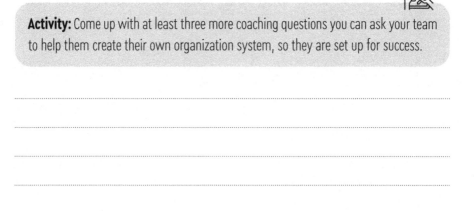

Activity: Come up with at least three more coaching questions you can ask your team to help them create their own organization system, so they are set up for success.

Setting the scene

Hamid is one of your low-productivity reps and it's beginning to affect his career prospects.

In this conversation, you want to paint a picture for Hamid so that he is clear on the cost to you and him of poor-time management and personal organization.

But you also want to highlight that there are clear benefits to getting his act together. You are going to review a typical day and explore his ideas to better plan and execute his priorities.

Coaching plan – preparation, conversation, application

Preparation – some things to consider before you coach Hamid:

- Observe Hamid in action for a week or longer and write your learnings down.

- Keep an open mind in case there are personal issues affecting his work life.

- Ask Hamid to keep a note/journal/record of what he plans vs. what gets done.

Reflection: What else will set you up for this conversation?

....

....

....

....

....

Conversation – some coaching questions to ask your rep(s):

- Walk me through your plan for this day/tomorrow.

- Walk me through your plan for this week.

- What are your key priorities for this week?

- How will you measure success this week?

- What does the ideal day look like for you?

- Where would managing your time help you to get better results?

- Which activities are draining your energy and motivation?

- What's the one thing that will free you up to get important things done?

- What will help you to focus on revenue-generating activities (RGAs)?

- Describe to me how you plan your calls/meetings/visits.

- Which things can you delete or delay or delegate so you can do what's important?

- How much time have you decided to dedicate to this activity this week?

- If you were in my shoes, where could I help you to be more productive/structured?

Activity: Come up with three more coaching questions you can ask Hamid here.

....

....

....

....

....

....

Application – next steps:

- Which steps could Hamid take to be better organized?

- How will you keep Hamid accountable for this activity?

- When will you follow up with him next?

....

....

....

....

....

Excerpt from sample coaching conversation

Conversation	Coaching analysis
You: Hey Hamid. Thanks for setting aside time in your calendar to have this 30-minute meeting. It's really important that you have all the support you need to organize yourself so you can be a success here. That's why I'm here.	*You have scheduled this meeting. You have not casually dropped in on Hamid because that would encourage the opposite of what you want him to do – manage his time. You allude to the fact that his success is linked to his ability to organize himself.*
Hamid: Hey! Sure. No problem.	
You: The clock is ticking. Let's get down to business [laughing] so we can end on time, and I can let you get back to your 3rd call block.	*A gentle reminder that time is important and that Hamid's call block is sacrosanct.*
Hamid: Sure.	

Conversation	Coaching analysis
You: As I explained in the calendar invite, my goal today is to ensure you are tracking to your revenue goals this week. When did you last check your KPIs?	*You confirm the importance to you of Hamid tracking to his goals.*
Hamid: Ehhh. Not today. I've been calling this list.	
You: I see. OK. How much time have you set aside this week to call prospects?	*You challenge Hamid's assumption of his priorities.*
Hamid: Do you mean the accounts I'm working? I'm calling them every day.	*Hamid confirms he is unclear about his priorities.*
You: OK. What else is on your list of priorities this week apart from that?	*You seek to understand how Hamid can rethink his priorities.*
Hamid: [Pauses to think and draws a blank].	
You: Would it help if I show you my plan for my week?	*You decide to lead by example and show how you are planning your week and establishing what is important to achieve.*
Hamid: Sure.	
You: So here on the left is my list of my top three priorities for this week. Here on the right are the timeslots when I will get these things done. You can see that I have set aside five one-hour blocks to cover what's critical to me. One of these blocks is you! Make sense?	*You explain a simple system and subtly let Hamid know that his planning (or the lack of it) is now on your radar.*
Hamid: Oh. OK.	

Conversation	Coaching analysis
You: [Pause] So do you make out a plan like this?	
Hamid: Not really. I just kind of… Not really	*Hamid confirms that he has no clear structure or system in place.*
You: It's really important to the business that we have reps who have a plan each day and for the week ahead. You are responsible for a chunk of revenue. That's why I think you're good enough to be in that chair. So, tell me: how will you measure your goals this week?	*You emphasize a system how the business measures success. You ask him about the value of having a system like this. You pay him a compliment.*
Hamid: My KPIs? My dials?	
You: So, your KPIs are an indication that you are tracking to goal. They are not your actual goals.	*You clarify the difference between goals and metrics.*
You: In the 20 minutes that we have remaining, why don't we do this? [You ask Hamid to create a five-day break-down of his week mapped to his three RGA (revenue generating activities) priorities measured by KPIs].	*You offer your guidance to help Hamid get organized.*
You: Great. That took us 15 minutes. How much time can you commit to doing this this week and every week from now on?	*You demonstrate that planning need not take very long. You make it clear that this is to be a new behavior from today.*
Hamid: 15 minutes. [Smiles] OK. I can do that.	
You: How will organizing yourself and sharing your plan with me for ten minutes help you?	*You check for understanding.*

Conversation	Coaching analysis
Hamid: It's going to help me land my sales goal. OK. I can do that.	
You: How about first thing after our daily stand up every Monday?	*You ask Hamid to commit to being kept accountable by sharing his plan every Monday.*
Hamid: Yeah. That would work. I don't start doing my calls until 8.30am.	*Hamid confirms that his schedule permits him to add this new weekly activity to the mix.*
You: Exactly. The reps who make it past the first year are those who make a habit of mapping out their plan each week. So, before we wrap up in the four minutes we have left, what are *your* three priorities for this week and when will *you* get them done?	*You stress that success in your team is linked to his habit of planning weekly. You ask him to teach back what he has agreed to and you ask him to confirm deadlines so he can be kept accountable.*
Hamid: [Confirms dates and times]	
You: We have another 30-minute check-in this week. Let's compare calendars now. When can you schedule me into your calendar, so it doesn't clash with your RGAs?	*You stress that Hamid has to take action by scheduling you in. It is not your responsibility to schedule him in. You remind him of prioritizing his RGAs.*

Closing ideas

Could you find out whether time management training has been offered and taken by your reps? Very often, new reps are full of enthusiasm with regards to selling but struggle with some of the basic skills, the most important of which are self-management and personal organization.

Could you enlist the help of more experienced reps by buddying them up with newer reps so they can learn to organize themselves on a daily and weekly basis before they learn anything about sales? This also takes the pressure off you so you can focus on higher priorities.

Could you work with HR/Talent Acquisition to screen-in reps who display high levels of self-management – and screen-out those who don't? It will always be easier on you if you hire people who have a demonstrable aptitude for planning. If you don't, you'll invariably end up nursing them and chasing them irrespective of how skilled they are.

Could you do a better job of leaning into time management and planning when you run your coaching sessions with your reps? What you coach is what your reps tend to pay attention to. When you make these behaviors a priority, people will learn to prioritize them too.

Not qualifying opportunities

It's truly amazing how many salespeople don't qualify properly. Even when they have been trained, they post opportunities in the CRM which have no chance of ever being closed.

They hope that opportunities will turn out for the best. But invariably, *anything half-qualified is unqualified.* And when your reps go to close unqualified deals, they collapse like a cheap deckchair.

Your role is to coach your reps to uncover gaps and assumptions and ask the hard questions early in the sales process, so they save themselves, you and the prospect later down the line. Anything half-qualified is unqualified.

Reflection: How well-qualified are the opportunities currently in your pipeline?

....

....

....

....

....

Anything half qualified is unqualified

. . . .

Wild goose chase

During my first three months as a BDR, probably as much as 40% of my leads did not meet the grade. I was hectic making sketchy calls, jumping on any old indication of a need and was ramming them into the CRM like crazy.

That's what you might call beginner's enthusiasm. At the end of month one, I was number three on the leader board and was very pleased with myself.

That was until just before quarter-end, when my field sales guy went to a string of meetings and found that they were mostly hot air. Naturally, he read me the riot act. I deserved his wrath.

I hadn't meant to deceive anyone. I simply hadn't applied myself to rigorously qualifying every meeting before sending him on a wild goose chase.

With an erratic approach to qualification, it's no surprise that a lot of sales teams have 'duds' in the pipeline and 'swings' in the forecast

So, why don't your reps qualify opportunities?

Well, that's the $2.86 million question. Here are a couple of reasons why:

- **Don't want to qualify.** They are afraid of qualifying in case they discover that an opportunity isn't real. Reps like this have a tendency not to ask too many 'hard questions' in case they get answers they don't like or can't get answers to the questions they need to ask.

- **Don't know how to qualify.** They do not know how to qualify because they have never been properly coached to use a qualification framework such as BANT, MEDDPIC, SPIN etc. It's hard to imagine a sales professional *thriving* in the job or *surviving* in the job unless they know how to thoroughly qualify opportunities in tandem with their defined sales process.

- **Don't need to qualify.** They think that they don't *need* to qualify *certain kinds* of opportunities. You typically see this when a deal is below a certain threshold (e.g., below 5K) or when the deal is of a certain type, e.g., a renewal on an existing account. Some reps assume that deals are 'in the bag' or don't need to be qualified. That's a classic mistake.

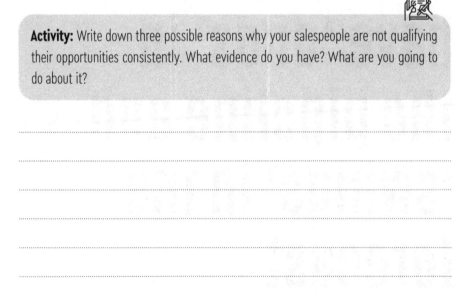

Activity: Write down three possible reasons why your salespeople are not qualifying their opportunities consistently. What evidence do you have? What are you going to do about it?

Instinct without inspection kills opportunity

It's practically impossible to overstate the need for rigorous qualification of every opportunity in your pipeline.

As you read this, I'm betting that many of your salespeople will occasionally 'wing' it while others use their 'gut instinct' (or some sixth sense) to decide if a 'lead' looks like a lead.

With an erratic approach like that, it's no surprise that a lot of enterprise sales organizations have 'duds' in the pipeline and wild swings in the forecast.

Qualification is your insurance policy

I like to think of sales qualification as a kind of insurance policy. It's going to save everyone a world of hurt further down the line.

When your reps are coached to always be qualifying (ABQ), it gives you and leadership the confidence that the *deal is real.* It confirms that your rep has done their due diligence and is having conversations with the right parties.

It also suggests that the opportunity has a superior chance of being closed.

In short, rigorous qualification confirms that it's worth investing your scarce resources and your people's time in pursuing an opportunity all the way through the gates, from prospect to 'closed won'.

When your reps are coached to ABQ (always be qualifying), it gives you and leadership the confidence that the *deal is real.*

Do a deal tear-down

Sit down with your AEs and do a 'deal tear-down' from top to bottom. Run a report in your CRM, pull out a couple of opportunities you want to *lift the lid on* and check them thoroughly.

A *deal tear-down* is where you go through an opportunity surgically. Rather than trying to find things to do, you are trying to find reasons to disqualify it or remove it from the pipeline through coaching.

Ask your AEs/SDRs/BDRS without warning to walk you and/or the team through one of their deals in play. Get them to put it on the screen and update you using your qualification framework.

Coach by asking powerful, direct questions. *Look for the pain*. Ask for validation. Are they just as proficient at qualifying out as they are at qualifying in?

Reflection: Who needs to be coached by you on qualification and why?

....

....

....

....

....

Don't let it slip back

Once you have trained your team up on something like MEDDIC, you need to coach your team relentlessly to ensure they don't slip back into the old way of qualifying (or not qualifying at all).

If that happens, there goes your return on training investment. So, start asking questions (suggestions below) to get your team to think about everything through your qualification framework.

From now on, absolutely every coaching conversation at every stage of the sales process revolves around qualification. Again and again and again.

Some questions to ask yourself

- Have we a qualification framework in place right now?

- Have my team been trained to apply it?

- Am I and my team leads reviewing all opportunities (or some) using it?

- Are we running forecast meetings using the framework?

- Is leadership speaking the same language as everyone else (e.g., MEDDIC)?

- Am I actively coaching all deal reviews through it?

- To what extent are we driving ABQ?

- How often do we have qualification masterclasses in our sales organization?

- How can new hires get the benefit of qualification training ASAP?

- How often do I hear the qualification framework mentioned on the sales floor?

Reflection: When did you last walk your reps through a model for a well-qualified opportunity

Coaching plan - preparation, conversation, application

Preparation – some things to consider:

- How well does my rep understand qualification?

- Which opportunity demands close inspection?

- What do I want my rep to focus on following this conversation?

▷|◁

Reflection: What else will set you up for a great conversation?

....

....

....

....

....

....

Conversation – some coaching questions to ask:

- What is the cost of this problem to your prospect right now?

- What is the compelling event that will drive this decision?

- How is this pain linked back to board-level initiatives?

- What happens if they don't take action this quarter?

- What is the expected return on investment (RoI) for this solution?

- How have you articulated value for this prospect?

- Where are you missing validated numbers?

- Who holds the pen to sign off on this initiative?

- Where does your economic buyer (EB) sit on the organization chart?

- What is the envisaged process from proof of concept (PoC) to implementation?

- How are procurement/legal involved in this process?

- Where are there likely to be bottlenecks and shortcuts?

Activity: Come up with at least three more coaching questions you can ask here.

....

....

....

....

....

....

Application – next steps:

- Which actions has your salesperson agreed to?

- How will you keep her/him accountable for this activity?

- When will you follow up with her next?

....

....

....

....

....

....

Setting the scene for coaching Frédérique

Frédérique has an unfortunate tendency to rely on opportunities that look good but have no real hope of crossing the finishing line. She is desperate to hit target.

Unfortunately, her deals tend to unravel despite her best efforts. You have done some research and reviewed her pipeline.

There is a whole bunch of things missing so you conclude that she is either unaware of what to ask or she is just not clear on the vital importance of qualifying opportunities properly.

Some tips to prepare for this coaching conversation

1. Have some concrete examples of opportunities that have not been properly qualified.

2. Review Frédérique's pipeline and inspect both early-stage and late-stage opportunities.

3. Review her training records to see whether she has been trained to qualify.

4. Consider which frameworks she has worked with in the past e.g., BANT, VIPP, SPIN, etc.

5. Ask Frédérique to select one of her opportunities and to *requalify it* before you see it.

Excerpt from sample coaching conversation

Conversation	Coaching analysis
You: Hi Frédérique. Things looking up?	*You detect some strain on Frédérique's face.*
Frédérique: Yes. Kind of. I know we've got 30 minutes set aside but can we make it 15?	*She wants to renege on the agreed time slot to review her deals. Fifteen minutes could be tight.*
You: That all depends, Frédérique. Why the change in plan?	*You suspect you know what's happening because qualification has been the subject of a recent one-to-one with Frédérique.*
Frédérique: Georges over at [company name] has just told me that it's not looking good. He isn't clear why the board are not gung-ho about our proposal. They were and now they're not. I really need to find out what the **** is going on.	*Frédérique is panicking because a past customer is having second thoughts about her latest proposal.*
You: OK. What do you think is going on?	*You invite Frédérique to collect her thoughts.*
Frédérique: I really don't know. Look. Can we take a rain-check on this?	*It appears that she has not an open channel of communication with her supposed Champion. Not a good sign. 'Rain-check' is not an option.*
You: Maybe I can help. Can you open this up in Salesforce really quick?	*You offer Frédérique the option of helping her with your perspective.*

Conversation	Coaching analysis
Frédérique: It's there on my screen. This is the solution they said they want and that's the solution they're currently using… and this is the proposal I've sent them.	*Frédérique has the bare minimum of data in Salesforce. There are a bunch of things missing. It's looking like a drive-by order rather than a qualified opportunity.*
You: Right. So, what did they say they are trying to fix exactly?	*You seek to understand the commercial imperative behind the opportunity aka the pain in the deal.*
Frédérique: We didn't cover that in detail. They said they were interested in our [name] solution. So, I put together a proposal for them.	*It looks like Frédérique has done it again. A proposal rushed out without any basis in fact. She has assumed that this would fly.*
You: Right. So, what is the business case for spending money with us?	*You ask Frédérique to clarify the exact business reason for engaging with your company.*
Frédérique: Like I said: we didn't cover that.	
You: Three questions for you. Write these down and let's answer them together. 1. What is the pain they are trying to fix? 2. Why fix it now? 3. Why are we the right ones to fix it?	*You need Frédérique to think carefully before she spends any more time (or yours) on this. You give Frédérique three simple questions to help her sense-check her proposal.*
Frédérique: I don't have this information.	*First problem.*
You: That's right you don't. [Pause]	*You feedback what you are hearing.*
Frédérique: What are you getting at?	
You: Would I be right in saying that there is no identified need here, Frédérique?	*You remind Frédérique of the ultra-importance of focusing first on the need so she's not throwing a solution over the fence.*

Conversation	Coaching analysis
Frédérique: Not exactly. But they were really interested. They like what our product does, and they want a demo.	*Frédérique doesn't appear to be getting the message. Spending time and resources on demos is a massive suck on business costs.*
You: And how what would our product help them to solve?	*You try again to get Frédérique to connect the dots between the pain and the solution to the pain.*
Frédérique: I didn't ask that. Georges was definitely interested so I closed him.	*Still not getting through. She is panicking.*
You: I got that. Interested. Let's rewind. Early on, when you are prospecting, you need to be qualifying, right? How would you define qualification?	*You start with a basic assessment of her understanding of qualification.*
Frédérique: It's seeing if they are a good fit for us and we are a good fit for them.	*Frédérique does understand it. She's just not applying it.*
You: Nicely put. Yeah.	*You congratulate her on her choice of definition.*
You: Which questions did you ask to ensure that they are a good fit for us and we are a right fit for them?	*You remind her of the importance of following the qualification framework.*
Frédérique: I actually didn't because they have bought from us before.	*OK. It appears that we have understood part of the issue.*
You: So you decided not to qualify Georges because they have bought from us before?	*You repeat Frédérique's exact choice of words back to her.*
Frédérique: Yes.	
You: So what is happening now?	

Conversation	Coaching analysis
Frédérique: They don't need it! (*****)	
You: Let's take it easy. We're going to go through this in detail from top to bottom. You're going to tell me what your options are then you're going to come up with a plan to jointly re-evaluate this with Georges. OK? Tell me where you want to start. OK?	*You switch gears from developmental coaching to directive coaching. Time is of the essence. Frédérique needs to cool down and save this opportunity. However, you are not taking over the steering wheel. This is her opportunity and her responsibility. You ask her to choose an option to start with.*
Frédérique: OK.	

Closing ideas

Some organizations flirt with qualification frameworks resulting in a mishmash of different and competing methods.

How can you ensure that everyone in your sales organization uses the one sales methodology and coaches to it?

Your sales process is the series of prospect interactions and meetings that must take place in an established order. It's designed to complement your customer's buying process.

How can you ensure that your sales team's qualification approach is aligned to your sales process?

Your reps need to be thoroughly qualifying every single opportunity. Otherwise, they stand to create problems for themselves (and you!) down the line.

How can you drive ABQ so that your reps get the message?

Reflection: Getting your salespeople to qualify opportunities properly is going to pay dividends down the line. What's your first step today?

Not telling stories

Facts tell, but stories sell

· · · · · · · · · · · · · · · · · · · ·

A salesperson's bank of stories does the hard work. Stories convince someone to listen to your salesperson, to talk to them, to answer questions and to take the next steps with them.

And the reason is that your mind and those of your customers are hard-wired for stories. Selling yourself, your brand and your business is inextricably linked with stories.

A story is a vehicle for all this information. It is a way to craft a message so that it lands with the person who hears it. Great stories are a shortcut in the minds of the listener.

A story should communicate proof of an idea. It should also create an emotional connection between the person telling the story and the person receiving it.

What has coaching storytelling to do with sales? Everything

Your brain likes stories

When your salesperson resorts to selling via fact-based information, they are engaging two individual parts of a prospect's brain known as *Wernicke's Area* and *Broca's Area*. These areas of the brain deal with language comprehension and language processing respectively.

But when your sales team tells stories, up to eight different parts of the listener's brain light up, including the areas responsible for colors, shapes, sounds, movement and touch. Your prospect's brain responds to the story as if the events communicated are happening to them.

Pitch a story not a product

Stories connect feelings with action. They paint a picture of what it feels like to own something and experience its benefits.

It's no surprise then those prospects are more likely to feel emotionally involved in what your salesperson is relaying to them when your salesperson pitches a story rather than a product.

Stories help my team build credibility fast. We don't let them near prospects until they can tell a story at every level of the product stack.

Rob Berry, Director of Inside Sales at NETSCOUT

Stories must be natural

If your people need to be coached on anything relentlessly and religiously, it's the stories they sell and their ability to sell through them. Keep in mind though, that we are not recommending people learning stories as a script.

You don't want people learning stories in a stilted, rehearsed manner. That's just false. It doesn't take a sophisticated listener to realize that they are being pitched a script. *Leave scripts to people who take orders in drive-thrus. OK?*

People want proof not product

The cold truth is that people don't want your product. They want the benefit of owning your product. They want proof that it will work for them because it has worked for people *just like them.*

The trouble is that not every salesperson is fluent in customer success metrics. They can't pivot in any situation and provide 'proof' at each stage of the buying conversation.

Instead, they resort to giving the same dump of features to anyone who will listen. Often, they sell the wrong message to the wrong person.

Your salespeople need three kinds of knowledge

1. **Product knowledge.** Salespeople are usually great at explaining their products. It's communicating helpful facts and information.

    Q: How well do your people know *what* they sell?

2. **Process knowledge.** This is how your salespeople learn to sell. It's the sales process they go through from discovery to close.

   Q: How well do your people know *how* to sell?

3. **Proof knowledge.** These are the stories that your salespeople need to know inside out so they can articulate business value.

   Q: How well do your people know *why* people buy?

Why not telling stories is a problem for you

Again and again, I hear sales managers say: *I really need these guys to be talking to the C-suite.* I need them to have bigger conversations with decision-makers. I get it.

But if you are wondering why your reps are hitting a *glass ceiling*, it is possibly (among other things) because they cannot build a *'staircase'* to the people they aspire to connect with.

They cannot craft (and deliver) a credible story that highlights how they have helped people in the C-suite. Facts tell but stories sell.

Connect quickly with the right story

Several years ago, after multiple calls, I unexpectedly got through to the CIO of a Fortune 50 company. There was some Irish American family connection.

We had a pleasant chat about the 'old country', but could I think of a credible 'proof' story to pitch, related to my product offering? Not a chance.

I was talking to a guy who had something personal in common. He really wanted to talk but I couldn't tell a story that would make him want to progress a commercial conversation.

I could tell *my* story, but I couldn't relate a *customer success story* of how someone just like him had benefited from setting up a next step with someone like me.

I should have had my story ready. Lesson learned.

▷|◁

Reflection: Think of the last time one of your team failed to 'connect' with someone highly influential. Coach them on the story they would tell if you had the chance to do it again?

....

....

....

....

....

....

If I don't buy you, I don't buy from you

. . . .

Are they audible-ready?

You spend valuable time trying to get your reps to have more value-driven, business-centric conversations with big-decision-makers.

So, what happens if they do get through? Are they *audible-ready?*

Can they pivot between taking to the C-suite and line managers? Can they switch between stories that resonate with technical people or gatekeepers?

Can they do so fluently and confidently?

What is the point of prospecting like crazy only to choke *when you get your chance to sing?* If you put your reps on the spot right now, how will they do?

Will they revert to talking facts *about* the product? Or can they tell stories that *sell* the product?

How good are they at using success stories that resonate with people?

▷|◁

Reflection: How confident are you around your team's ability to relate powerful, motivating stories that highlight the proof of your products and services? When did you last 'test' this in coaching?

Is your team fluent in the language of success?

. . . .

Some questions to ask yourself

- What have I done to create a storytelling framework for my team?

- Are my guys familiar with the case studies on our own website?

- Which kinds of activities can I run to coach storytelling?

- How can I champion storytelling against our playbook?

- How can we use stories to get past strategic objections?

- How can we use storytelling to overtake the competition?

- What can I do to get my guys to develop persona?

- Just how *audible-ready* are my team to reel off the right stories?

- How are we integrating stories into our onboarding?

- What degree of importance are we attaching to storytelling culturally?

- Do I as a sales leader *lead* with examples of stories?

Reflection: What else do you need to ask yourself before you coach?

Coaching plan – preparation, conversation, application

Preparation – some things to consider:

- How well does my rep tell the right stories?

- How well does my salesperson convince people to trust them?

- Where is the 'bank' of high-value stories you coach people on?

▷|◁

Reflection: What else will set you up for this conversation?

....

....

....

....

....

....

Conversation – some coaching questions to ask:

- *How do you convince people to trust you?*

- *Which story will resonate with technical stakeholders?*

- *Which story will make sense to legal stakeholders?*

- *Describe a time when we solved a problem like X.*

- *What have we done recently for companies in X vertical?*

- *Which challenge do we solve for X kinds of businesses?*

- *In X words, how can we provide value for companies like X?*

- *Which story would best illustrate our ability to do X?*

- *Give me an example of clients who can say X about us?*

- *Where do we help companies who have X problem?*

- *What is the consequence for prospects who can't do X?*

- *Which language would a CEO use to describe X?*

- *Which customer success story would resonate with a CEO Head of X?*

- *If I'm a prospect and say I'm struggling with X, which story would you tell?*

- *What's your favorite story of a time when we helped someone achieve X?*

- *How could you improve/tighten-up/share this story?*

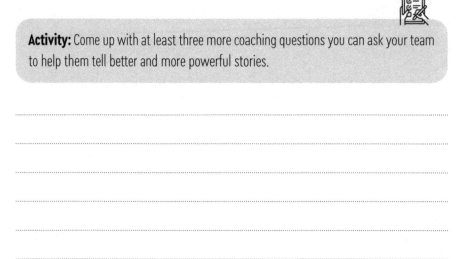

Activity: Come up with at least three more coaching questions you can ask your team to help them tell better and more powerful stories.

Application – next steps:

- Which actions has your salesperson agreed to?

- How will you keep them accountable for this activity?

- When will you follow up with them next?

....

....

....

....

....

....

Setting the scene for coaching Sarah on storytelling

One of your reps has an important call with a CEO she needs to convince. There is a lot riding on this meeting and Sarah feels that regurgitating a pitch deck of slides won't work. She thinks that crafting a good story will help her get through to her prospect's values.

You use your coaching to help Sarah come up with a powerful example using the story-selling framework she has been trained on. It's rather short notice so you have to get her to think and take action.

Some tips to prepare for this coaching conversation

1. Resist the temptation to tell Sarah which approach to take.

2. Refresh your memory of the stories so that you know them first.

3. Offer to help if you are available.

4. Check whether she has been trained on storytelling.

5. Walk Sarah through all the steps of your storytelling framework.

Excerpt from sample coaching conversation

Conversation	Coaching analysis
You: What's up Sarah?	*Sarah looks like she's a little stressed.*
Sarah: Busy morning. I've got this 14.30 call with the CEO over at [company name]. That's in four hours.	
You: Cool. How are you feeling about it? Are you ready?	*You wonder if she should not be feeling more confident. Quick verbal check to find out where Sarah's mindset is at.*
Sarah: Kind of…	
You: OK. What does *kind of* mean?	*You check Sarah's choice of words.*
Sarah: I haven't spoken to this woman before. So, I've been told that she's a super-instinctive decision-maker. I checked out her LinkedIn profile using *Crystal Knows* and that seems to check out.	*You discover the source of Sarah's angst.*
You: What checks out?	*You seek to clarify 'check-out'.*
Sarah: So, it looks like she's not allergic to detail. But she doesn't want a whole dump of technical information either. My read is that she'll like me, or she won't. She'll like our brand, or she won't.	*Sarah gives her synopsis of the prospect's thinking process and her chances of connecting her.*
You: OK. Got it. So, your *read* is that she's going to make a decision that is *instinctive*. It sounds like you believe she will make an emotional decision as much as a logical decision.	*You play her words back to her and give her feedback on what you have heard to sense-check it.*
Sarah: I don't really know. I've decided to park the slides. Her CTO has already got those. I'll keep them but I won't lead with them.	

Conversation	Coaching analysis
You: What could you try that might resonate with someone like that based upon your *read* of your prospect?	*You help Sarah to think through what her options are, and you use her word back to her.*
Sarah: The first thought I had over coffee was that I need to wow her with a powerful story of what we have achieved for [company Y]. We crushed that last project and Sanjay was able to build a narrative that resonated with decision-makers. The solution was going to shore up defences against compliance risks. By weaving business-case metrics, customer-proof metrics and technical metrics into a powerful customized story, Sanjay got the green light for the $200K project.	*Sarah recalls the benefits of a story that might just be appropriate to lead with.*
You: OK. So why that example?	*You check whether it's the appropriate example.*
Sarah: It's the same industry and almost a mirror of the outcomes that my Champion says are important to the CEO at a strategic level.	*Sarah confirms that she is happy with her choice of story for her prospect.*
You: How will you structure that story based upon the framework we covered in our story-selling training?	*You coach Sarah to think through her story pitch based upon story-selling training she has had.*
Sarah: OK. The challenge from that example is that Sanjay's VP of Infrastructure was concerned about data vulnerability. At the time we spoke to Sanjay, he had learned that they were non-compliant with federal data protection requirements for health care providers. There were facing potential massive penalties.	*Sarah gives her take on the challenge part of her story.*

Conversation	Coaching analysis
You: How can you align those challenges with what this CEO is facing from her board so that she can see the relevant parallels?	*You remind Sarah of the importance of aligning the pains of her prospect with those of the subject in the story.*
Sarah: [Sarah responds]	*[Sarah pulls out two specific examples that match her prospect's situation]*
You: You've covered two things. Is there anything else?	*You help Sarah to consider whether there is anything else to lean into.*
Sarah: Oh yeah. I need to include the results from [product name] too.	*Sarah jumps prematurely to the end of the story.*
You: Good point. We'll come to the results part of your story shortly. What about the solution which we implemented? Why is that the appropriate solution to relate to your prospect in this situation?	*You gently bring her back to the middle or 'solution' part of her story so that she aligns the correct product with the results she believes will match the prospect's needs.*
Sarah: [Sarah responds]	
You: Now what are the results? You said that *this is almost a mirror of the outcomes that your Champion says are important to the CEO at a strategic level.* Did I get that right?	*You coach Sarah to sense-check the appropriate outcomes and remind her of the importance of aligning them with the CEO. You use her exact words back to her.*
Sarah: Well, that's my understanding.	*Sarah doesn't sound like she is 'audible-ready' to pitch the story to the prospect.*
You: Have you walked your Champion through the storyline you are going to pitch to the CEO?	*You check in whether Sarah has lever-aged her Champion to help her master the story.*
Sarah: No. I haven't. That's a good shout. I'll see if I can get him on the phone now.	*Sarah realizes she could do with her Champion's help and confirms the action she needs to take.*

Conversation	Coaching analysis
You: OK. Noted. When you've done that, what's going to get you feeling comfortable between now and 14.30?	*You indirectly remind Sarah that she has a deadline to meet but needs to sound relaxed.*
Sarah: I think I need to practice it so it sounds natural and so that I am hitting the right value-markers. I also need feedback on how it sounds.	*Sarah confirms that she needs to get things right and will need some help.*
You: So how can I help?	*You ask if she feels she needs help. It is up to her to prioritize it and ask for it.*
Sarah: Can we do a role-play?	
You: First, I've a call with Sean [VP of Sales] in 15 minutes. Don't want to bump Sean! [Laughing]. Let's take 30 minutes at 12.30 to go over *your* story so *you* are primed.	*You remind Sarah of your priorities and your need to attend to them first. When it suits your calendar, you are free to offer her a 30-minute slot that works for you both.*
You: So, to summarize, you're going to check in with your Champion immediately to get their take. What else?	*You conclude by playing back the steps that Sarah has chosen to take.*
Sarah: I'm going to refine my story points so we can role-play this at 12.30. That's the lot for now.	*Sarah sums up her actions.*
You: Done. See you at 12.30 in meeting room 6. I'll take care of booking that.	*You wrap up and free Sarah up to focus on her actions by booking the room for you both.*
Sarah: Thanks for your time.	

Closing ideas

Great storytellers are great story-sellers. So, what are your thoughts now to make storytelling part of your sales culture?

Could you instigate storytelling training for your team as well as the wider go-to-market organization? If you want to see your team embracing this new skill, they are probably going to need some formal training through a workshop.

Could you integrate storytelling into your one-to-ones and team meetings on a consistent basis? Storytelling/story-selling is a fundamental skill of all great communicators and salespeople.

Could you leverage *Slack* or your sales organization channels to champion great exchanging of stories? It makes sense that there is a flow of good-news stories between customer success, account management, inside sales, pre-sales as well as your SDRs, XDRs, BDRs, AEs, etc.

▷|◁

Reflection: How are you going to put storytelling front and centre in your sales team's coaching and enablement? Come up with three ideas now.

....

....

....

....

....

Not following the sales process

Salespeople are (usually) trained to *use* a sales process. But the question you must ask yourself is whether your team are *following* that sales process.

The sales process is your company's way of selling. It's the recipe for success. It's the sales journey that your team serve customers from beginning to end.

Getting your team to stick to the sales process

Your sales process is not a road. That would suggest that your people can take detours. The process is more like a sales track or set of rails to a destination.

So, it's vital that your sales reps understand what each stop on the journey looks like, so they can find out where each prospect is on the track. OK?

Don't assume your team follow the sales process

Prospects might be further along the journey when they board. Not everyone is at the discovery stage. Some *board the train* at the demo or PoC stage.

But that's no excuse to not to requalify prospects as if they are boarding the train at the first stop.

Trouble starts when your salesperson assumes everyone knows where they are in the journey, and no one 'checks the tickets'. Agreed?

Don't let your team take shortcuts

So, if your sales process is clear and logical, why don't your reps follow it? Some reps think they don't need to follow it. They take shortcuts.

The sales process has been designed to get everyone to the next stop. When your people take shortcuts, *the wheels come off* the train.

Your sales process has been designed to take the guesswork out of the system

· · · · · · · · · · · · · · · · · · ·

Why it matters

Any competent salesperson should be able to sell your products and services if they follow your sales process and the steps in each stage.

As the VP of Sales for a Seattle-based SaaS company told me: *I could make a salesperson out of anyone if they just follow the sales process. We know it works. When my team don't follow the sales process, what's the point of giving them leads?*

Guesswork is bad work

Your sales process has been designed to take the guesswork *out* of the system.

So, when you've got reps who jump stages and take shortcuts, *that puts the guesswork back into the system.* Good luck forecasting that.

▷|◁

Reflection: Which of your reps is following the sales process and which ones aren't? Why not? What could you do get them to want to follow it?

....

....

....

....

....

....

Some questions to ask yourself

- Do we have a defined sales process in place?

- If I ask any of my reps to explain it to me, am I happy with the answer?

- When I spot-check a deal in pipeline, is it typically at the right process stage?

- Is our sales process too long/convoluted/easy to follow?

- When did the guys last get some training on our sales process?

- How does our sales process map to our average customer's buying process?

- Which stages of our process are my reps typically strongest at?

- Which stages of our process see me having to do the most coaching?

- Where in the sales process do most opportunities get stuck?

- What (if anything) is preventing my guys from updating after each engagement?

- Do we have a sales playbook that supports our sales process step-by-step?

- How do I know my team are clear on each stage of the sales process?

- Do we have a cheat-sheet which our reps can refer to?

- Are the team clear on how to follow-up if the outcome is closed/lost?

▷|◁

Reflection: What else do you need ask yourself? Any thoughts as you read the list?

Coaching plan - preparation, conversation, application

Preparation – some things to consider before you start:

- What can I do to communicate the importance of the sales process?

- How well does my rep generally stick to the sales process?

- Which opportunities can I highlight and coach on?

Reflection: What else will set you up for this conversation?

....

....

....

....

....

....

Conversation – questions you can ask your rep in coaching:

- *Describe to me what happens at each stage of the sales process.*

- *What happens at discovery stage for you to mark it complete?*

- *How do you know the prospect has passed the qualification stage?*

- *Which stage of the sales process are you most comfortable with?*

- *Which part of the sales process do you struggle with a little?*

- *What do you need to justify arranging a PoC?*

- *Which stage of the process are most of your opps at right now?*

- *When do you typically update the CRM with conversation notes?*

- *How do you decide on the probability stage of your opportunities?*

- *When did you last run a report in the CRM?*

- *What do you do before moving an opp from proposal to negotiation?*

- *Where in the sales process would gather information about budget?*

Activity: Come up with three more coaching questions you can ask here.

Application – next steps:

- Which actions has your salesperson agreed to?

- How will you keep them accountable for this activity?

- When will you follow up with her next?

....

....

....

....

....

....

Setting the scene for coaching Mahmoud

In this coaching conversation, you are checking in with Mahmoud. You notice that a lot of his opportunities are 'stuck' at prospecting stage even though they are marked at 70% probability.

You also notice that they are missing a lot of data which should be present to substantiate the opportunity. Finally, the closing date for several of his larger details is the end of the month, which appears to you to be totally unrealistic.

Mahmoud likes to leave it to the last minute to update his opportunities. You decide to coach him on some of these points.

Some tips to prepare for this coaching conversation

- Review notes from your last coaching session with Mahmoud.

- Run a report in your CRM to spot the stage(s) where most opps are.

- Pull opportunities to highlight a good/problematic example.

- Consider the conclusion you expect Mahmoud to arrive at.

- Set aside time to go through all opportunities in the closing motion.

- Ask Mahmoud to review the sales process stage for specific opps.

Excerpt of sample coaching conversation

Conversation	Coaching analysis
You: Hi, Mahmoud. Are you well?	*Greet Mahmoud and inquire how he is doing to gauge his mood.*
Mahmoud: Hi, Mark. Good! How's things?	
You: Busy morning, Mahmoud! So, thanks for making time in your calendar to meet with me. Your EoQ [end of quarter] is fast approaching, and I think we can use the next 30 minutes to review some of your opps so you can get them over the line.	*Acknowledge and convey the urgency of the situation as EoQ is approaching. Clarify the objective and benefit of the session to Mahmoud.*
Mahmoud: Sounds good to me	
You: So, I've run a report in Salesforce and pulled several. These are the same ones I mailed you about at CoB [close of business] yesterday. Let's start with your prognosis. Where are these in terms of our sales process and what's the plan to close them?	*Remind Mahmoud of the email sent to outline what you will both cover. Invite him to give you a synopsis of the stage of the relevant opportunities in the CRM and ask him to explain his close plan.*
Mahmoud: OK. These ones here and here are closing next week. They're going to sign... probably Thursday or Friday. Whichever.	*Mahmoud's analysis is anything but a proper walk-through. In fact, it's sounding rather sketchy.*

Conversation	Coaching analysis
You: So if I have understood you, you're saying that they are *probably* going to sign next week. What makes you use the word *probably*?	*You check for understanding. You repeat Mahmoud's exact words back to him and you seek to clarify his choice of the word 'probably'.*
Mahmoud: They're as good as closed.	
You: OK. So, they're both down as *prospecting*?	*You challenge the incongruity. If the prospect is going to sign next week, why is the opp at 'prospecting' stage? You invite him to correct the anomaly.*
Mahmoud: Mmmm.	
You: Given that they're closing next week, where do you think they should be?	
Mahmoud: Probably negotiating?	*Mahmoud is asking you to decide. There's that word 'probably' again.*
You: You tell me. This is your prospect. So, what's your action here?	*You indicate it's his decision.*
Mahmoud: To update them. OK. I should have done that.	*Mahmoud understands the issue.*
You: Let's write that down now as an action so we have some clear next steps at the end of my visit today.	*You challenge Mahmoud to come up with his first action point.*
You: Got that down? Great. Question for you: When should an opportunity be moved from prospecting to *qualification*?	*You prompt him to prepare to discover more. You check for his knowledge of the difference between the first two stages in the sales process.*
Mahmoud: [Answers]	

Conversation	Coaching analysis
You: Good. And what kinds of information does the playbook tell you that you need to confirm with your prospect/Champion to move this forward?	*You congratulate him on getting the answer right and hint at what he should be using and whom he should be verifying sales intelligence with on the buyer's side.*
Mahmoud: [Answers]	
You: Good! And what is the consequence if I run a report for my forecast and these are incorrect?	*You check whether he understands the implication of the sales process not being followed.*
Mahmoud: [Pause] The forecast is incorrect too.	
You: It's not good for me and it's not good for you. [Pause and silence]	*You let this linger in Mahmoud's mind and pause for effect.*
You: Here's the thing, Mahmoud. It worries me that several of these are down as *prospecting* when you seem to know that this isn't accurate. You just said *I should have done that.* [Pause and silence]	*You gently warn Mahmoud that he is not following the sales process… and he knows it.*
Mahmoud: You're right.	
You: So, let me ask you this: When should you be updating these records?	*You take note of Mahmoud's answer because you will be emailing him a record of this conversation. This will be going in your coaching journal for follow-up action for you.*
Mahmoud: Right away. I just kind of left it. I'll do them now.	
You: Nope. Park that for later. I've got nine actions from reviewing these opps on *my* time. You've got a 9.30 with [prospect name]. Before we wrap up, what are your next steps?	*You allow Mahmoud to come to his own conclusions and action points. You remind him he has a hard-stop.*

Closing questions for you

- How could you clarify which training your reps get on the sales process?

- How happy are you with your team's understanding of the sales process?

- How can you use coaching to ensure adherence to the sales process?

▷|◁

Reflection: What tells you your salespeople are following your sales process right now?

Not forecasting

You need visibility

If your salespeople are unable to get to grips with even basic forecasting, they are likely to be unable to provide you with visibility around the quality of their pipeline.

You need a brand

How can you possibly present your numbers to sales leadership if there is no certainty around them? Your brand as a leader is at stake if your reps cannot provide you with credible numbers.

You need trust

It also says something about their relationship with you. When your reps feel like they don't have to load the numbers or tweak them, they are more likely to be forthright and honest with themselves.

If your salespeople's forecasts don't stack up, yours won't stack up either

Why does this happen? Forecasting myths

I ran a workshop recently for two groups of newly promoted sales leaders and detected a little bit of apprehension. No surprise. Many sales professionals – even those in senior positions – baulk at the idea of forecasting.

Why is this the case?

- Myth 1: It's shrouded in some mathematical mystique which make it difficult.

- Myth 2: It's the language of senior managers or those who sit in board meetings.

- Myth 3: It's got nothing to do with me… I'm just a… (add job title here).

Let's take that last myth first. Forecasting means having confidence in your version of the future and being able to stand over it. If your salespeople are engaged in activities which have a direct effect on future revenue, it has *everything* to do with them.

Next, forecasting is less about the maths and more about giving you a level of predictability. It certainly isn't the language of senior leaders only.

Forecasting concerns everyone

An account executive does not have to produce detailed forecasts to the same depth that a manager does. That said, your sales organization is a team.

If the junior members of the team aspire to become senior members of the team, they should at the very least be familiar with forecasting basics.

- What forecasting is.
- How it works.
- Why sales needs it.

Warren Buffett is alleged to have said: *Forecasts may tell you a great deal about the forecaster; they tell you nothing about the future.*

Forecasts are not a guarantee of the future, but they are a useful exercise in helping you to understand the psychology, reliability, and credibility of your salespeople. Forecasting is everyone's business.

Activity: Write down three possible reasons why your salespeople are not forecasting or showing any interest in the consequences of forecasting.

....

....

....

....

....

....

Forecasting as a coaching opportunity

You don't want to put your rep under the microscope, but you do want to put their numbers under the microscope.

When forecasting is an issue, you want to challenge assumptions and gaps. You want to use coaching to ensure that the maths and reality tell the right story.

As a sales leader, your role is to get your people focused on doing the things that will paint a realistic picture so you can report the right numbers.

Some questions to ask yourself

- How consistently are your reps able to predict their results?

- Does everyone share the same understanding of terms used?

- When did team last get training on forecasting and was it evaluated?

- What does someone's reluctance to commit tell me about mindset?

- To what extent are my reps over-optimistic about their numbers?

- What tells me my reps are telling me what they think I want to hear?

- What tells me that my team feel safe discussing bad news with me?

- Which of my reps tend to kick deals into the following quarter?

- Why are some of my reps falling short of their predictions?

- What tells me they focus on large deals over small deals or vice versa?

- What is going on in the CRM that needs closer inspection?

- To what extent is my rep relying on clear facts or hearsay/opinion?

- How often am I checking in with my reps on important deals?

▷|◁

Reflection: What else do you need to consider at this point?

....

....

....

....

....

....

Setting the scene for coaching Tamsin

Tamsin's forecast was a bit *lumpy* again. Some months her forecasts were target. Other months, they were way off the mark.

You believed that Tamsin needed to do a much better job of forecasting.

You wanted her to realize that her forecast accuracy (or the lack of it) was affecting you when you reported to leadership.

It was also affecting her credibility in the organization and her career prospects.

Tamsin wanted to work her way up to sales manager. She was already trained on how to forecast. So, if she wanted that leadership position, she had to start to develop her skills. This last bit of information could give you leverage.

You asked Tamsin some basic questions:

- *How does forecasting concern you in your role?*

- *What's holding you back from forecasting with confidence?*

- *How will this skillset help you in future roles?*

As Tamsin opened up, you heard her explain that she was unaware how important forecasting was to her and to you (as her sales leader).

So, you brought up the question of her career next steps and related a story of how it helped you when you stepped into the role of a manager.

- Tamsin was now crystal clear that forecasting was her responsibility.

- She realized that her numbers were a little shaky and needed tightening.

- Tamsin discovered that she needed coverage to come in on target.

Tamsin asked for some one-to-one time with you so she could improve her technique, and you scheduled some time in your diary to help her.

Coaching plan – preparation, conversation, application

Preparation – some things to consider before you coach Tamsin:

- Inspect Tamsin's pipeline and pull out a spread of opportunities.

- Review the trends of Tamsin's predictions versus results.

- Check records to see if Tamsin has been trained to forecast.

▷|◁

Reflection: What else will set you up for this conversation?

....

....

....

....

....

Conversation – questions you can ask Tamsin in coaching:

- *What's your definition of commit/upside/likely?*

- *Walk me through the business case for X opportunity.*

- *Walk me through how you came up with this number.*

- *What is the decision-stage for X opportunity?*

- *What's left to be done to get these key opportunities over the line?*

- *What are some of the risks that you need to be thinking about?*

- *Where are you feeling unsure with regards to your numbers?*

- *Which detail/metrics/projections have you been unable to clarify?*

- *If there was one thing to give you more certainty, what is it?*

- *What's your plan to hit your number in case these deals fall through?*

- *Where do you need coverage, so you come in on target?*

- *What would give you more confidence to forecast better?*

Activity: Come up with three more coaching questions you can ask here.

....

....

....

....

....

Application – next steps:

- Which steps has Tamsin agreed to take so she can forecast better?
- How will you keep Tamsin accountable for this activity?
- When will you follow up with her next?

....

....

....

....

....

....

Excerpt from sample coaching conversation

Conversation	Coaching analysis
You: Hi, Tamsin. Welcome back from vacation.	
Tamsin: Thanks. We had a great time. I really needed that break so I can get my head clear and focus on hitting my number in Q4.	*Tamsin is back and refreshed.*
You: Glad you got the break. Speaking of numbers, can you please put some time in your calendar this week?	*You want Tamsin to get a clear steer on her forecast numbers.*
Tamsin: Sure. What's up?	
You: I've decided to ask you and the team to present your numbers to leadership from now on rather than just to me.	*You want the team to be confident enough to listen to feedback from peers because the forecast affects the business.*
Tamsin: OK. Well now is as good a time as any.	*Tamsin appreciates that salespeople should be intimately familiar with their numbers.*

Conversation	Coaching analysis
You: I've got 15 minutes now, but we'll need to schedule a deeper dive by Thursday. Ordinarily, I would want you to go through all the steps we covered in the forecasting training back in April.	*You don't just want to gather Tamsin's numbers; you want to understand how she arrived at these numbers. The team have all been through training.*
You: Let's think of the next 15 minutes as a refresher and focus on your commit number. What's your definition of *commit*?	*You decide to get Tamsin's understanding of the all-important commit number.*
Tamsin: It's an opportunity which I am confident will close in-quarter.	*Tamsin's on the right path.*
You: That's my definition too, Tamsin. Thanks. If we take an opportunity as *commit*, what might stand in the way of it not closing?	*You want to clarify further.*
Tamsin: Perhaps something unpredictable. But if the deal is well-qualified, it should only be a delay.	*Tamsin shares her view.*
You: What makes you say that?	*But what's her rationale?*
Tamsin: If I have something down as *commit*, it should be a safe bet. It should be properly qualified and linked to a compelling need to be closed in-quarter. I should have a confirmed timeline, sign-off and there should be as little as possible standing between the commitment and a signed contract.	*Tamsin shares her definition.*
You: OK. So, which of your opportunities meets the criteria you have just outlined?	*You ask her to apply her definition to her forecast.*

Conversation	Coaching analysis
Tamsin: I'm feeling good about Barnes Widgets Inc.	
You: When you say you are *feeling good*, what gives you the confidence that this is going to close?	*You want Tamsin to be more specific, so you ask her to qualify 'feeling good'.*
Tamsin: My decision-maker has given me a verbal go-ahead and we should *have ink* by Friday.	*Tamsin is willing to stand over Barnes Widgets.*
You: OK. So is this the only one you have in *commit*?	*You know that there is something else.*
Tamsin: There is one more opportunity in *commit* but over the break, I began to think whether it should belong in *probable*.	*Tamsin is now questioning her own predictions. This is good.*
You: OK. What are your thoughts?	*You direct the question/decision back to her.*
Tamsin: Samson Widgets Inc. fell into my lap a week before I went on leave. It's a renewal. I put it in *commit* but over vacation, I realized I'm missing a firm 'yes'.	*She has reasoned that this opportunity needs to be reclassified.*
You: What's left to be done to get this over your line?	*You ask her for her plan/next steps.*
Tamsin: I need to connect with the decision-maker to confirm that they have decided to go with us. Their last email says they'll come back to me. They've just got to get procurement to sign. Andy thinks it's a formality. But he's new.	*Tamsin responds.*
You: Does that sound like it belongs in commit?	*You sense-check her thinking.*
Tamsin: Mmm.	

Conversation	Coaching analysis
You: Are you happy presenting this to the team?	*The big question.*
Tamsin: No.	
You: So, what's your revision?	*You help her to get unstuck.*
Tamsin: I'm going to ask them for a decision and I'm going to put this in *probable*.	*Tamsin's response shows she's thinking along the right lines.*
You: What's your plan for coverage?	*You want to know that Tamsin has a plan B.*
Tamsin: Are you asking what my plan B is to hit my number in case Samson doesn't close?	*You know Tamsin already has a plan B.*
You: Yup.	*You switch to directive coaching to get Tamsin into action.*
Tamsin: I'm working on Linda Widgets Inc. That's one I'm excited about.	*Tamsin has a plan, and it sounds like she's on top of things.*
You: Great. I need you to go over *all* these numbers because everybody's presenting to Selena Monday week. We're holding a dry-run on Thursday morning. What are your next steps?	*You stress the importance of being ready to present and get her to confirm her commitment.*
Tamsin: I'm going to review the numbers and make sure they stack up with a clear plan for key opportunities.	*Tamsin shares her next steps.*
You: Thanks, Tamsin. Welcome back. The break has done you good.	

Closing questions for you

- How can I make forecasting simple and easy to execute?

- What do forecasts tell me about my team's thinking, not just their selling?

- What does the quality of my forecasts say about my sales leadership?

Reflection: What are your takeaways from this chapter and how will you apply them to your next forecasting check-in?

What now?

Congratulations are in order. You have reached the end of the book.

It doesn't matter whether you took a shortcut from the front page to get here.

This book was not designed to be read by you in one sitting.

- ✓ You can dip in and out when you need some ideas.
- ✓ You can turn to the relevant parts and get practical help.
- ✓ You can take the ideas you like and make them your own.

Coaching is leadership in its truest form so be prepared to get stuck in, try things out and be curious.

- ✓ You will be a better salesperson.
- ✓ You will be a better sales manager.
- ✓ You will be a better sales leader.

Start today!

You can also watch the free videos listed at the front of the book to get even more inspiration.

If you would like to work with us, visit www.salescoachr.com now to get more information.

Extras

Appendix 1

Coaching questions using qualification frameworks

B elow are some question sets which you can use depending on which framework you are using.

These are questions which you can take, tweak and try out. These are not for your reps to ask your prospects. These are here to help you coach your team.

You need to ask these continuously in all kinds of opportunities including meetings (see Part 2 of this book).

There is any number of ways of asking these kinds of questions (see Part 1 of this book).

What you will notice from reviewing the list below is that they are not designed to be easy-to answer and there is no 'one way' to answer them.

I invite you to use the questions to help your rep to challenge their own assumptions, spot information gaps and then come up with a plan to close them.

You will notice that there is some overlap between these question sets. That's OK. To some extent, most qualification frameworks use the same inspiration for questions.

That said, something like MEDDIC is typically used in consultative selling into Enterprise Sales organizations where there can be multiple parties involved in the buying process.

BANT questions

Coaching budget questions

- How much are they budgeting for this solution?
- Will this come out of their Q4 or Q3 budget?
- What did they say they are looking to invest?
- What is their ceiling for a project of this type?
- Have they ever gone over budget on a project like this?

Coaching authority questions

- Who makes financial decisions over there?
- What power has this person to sign off on projects like this?
- Are they the only person who will approve this?
- What did you ask to clarify they are a decision-maker/influencer/user?
- Who will be using/testing/approving this project?

Coaching need questions

- Where are they running into hurdles with their current vendor?
- What is the burning platform or main issue here?
- What happens if they don't action this in this quarter?
- How is the party you spoke to affected by this issue?
- How will this solution help them to increase efficiency/reduce costs, etc.?

Coaching timing questions

- When are they looking to push the button on this initiative?
- What makes you think this is something they will decide this month?
- How long have they been looking for a solution?

- When do they want/need/expect to have this in place?

- When do they hope to have a PoC in place?

MEDD(P)IC questions

Coaching metric questions

- What is the expected RoI for this solution?

- How have you articulated value for this prospect?

- What will the effect of this solution be on EBITDA/share price?

- What are the deal-size metrics that tell you it's got enough margin for us?

- How will a deal of this size contribute to your Q1 number?

- Where are you missing validated numbers?

- Where are you having issues with converting features to quantifiable benefits?

- Will this be coming out of Opex or Capex?

Coaching economic buyer questions

- Who holds the pen to sign off on this initiative?

- What is their power to make discretionary budget decisions?

- Where does your EB sit on the organization chart?

- How do you know your EB isn't part of a committee?

Coaching decision process questions

- What is the envisaged process from PoC to implementation?

- How are procurement involved in this process?

- Where are legal involved in this process?

- Where are the technical decision-makers in this process?

- Where are there likely to be bottlenecks and shortcuts?

- Have you reviewed any MSA/EULA?

- How will they evaluate the PoC?

- Which other PoCs are they running?

- What do you not yet know at this stage of the buyer's process?

- Who have you not yet talked to yet and why?

- How do you know they are not working with external consultants?

- What is the mutually agreed closing plan that reflects all stages of the process?

- How many signatures are there and what is the plan to get them?

Coaching decision criteria questions

- What are you doing to validate these criteria with your Champion?

- What is your plan to influence these criteria?

- Which part of the organization do these criteria come from?

- Which part of the decision criteria do we not measure up against?

- How are we being measured against the competition?

- How far along is the technical committee in the decision-making process?

- What will it take to get 'do nothing' off the table?

- How can we work with Pre-Sales to stack-rank these features?

- How do you know we are not part of a line-up at this stage?

Coaching identified pain questions

- What is the cost of this problem to your prospect right now?

- What is the compelling event that will drive this decision?

- How is this pain linked back to board-level initiatives?

- What happens if they don't take action this quarter?

- How/where does this problem manifest itself with the greatest effect?
- What does this prevent the board/senior leadership from executing?

Coaching Champion questions

- How have you identified/built/tested/used your Champion?
- When is your next check-in with your Champion?
- What kinds of similar projects has your Champion been involved in?
- What is their track record/success on initiatives like this one?
- Which kinds of information has your Champion not been able to get you?
- How has your Champion connected dots to the EB's pain points – not theirs?
- What is your Champion doing about getting you in front of the EB?
- How are they helping you to build a business case?
- How is your Champion justifying our involvement at this stage?

SPIN questions

Coaching situation questions

- What are they currently struggling with most?
- What system do they have in place in that department?
- How long have they been living with this problem?

Coaching problem questions

- Which of these issues are costing them the most money/people?
- How have you quantified the issue in terms of customer pain?
- How can you quantify churn in this department?

Coaching implication questions

- When you follow the pain, where does it have the greatest effect?

- What does this problem lead to higher up the food chain?

- What is this issue doing to their bottom line?

Coaching need questions

- What kind of solution could we help them to build?

- Which of these areas are they going to try to fix first?

- What are they likely to want to prioritize?

Appendix 2

Training versus coaching

Training	Coaching
New information	Existing information
From external sources	From internal source
Typically one-to-many	Typically one-to-one
Often monologue	Must be a dialogue
Trainer usually is a subject matter expert	Coach need not be an expert
Task-focused	Person-focused
Usually one-off	Continuous in nature
No interpersonal trust required	Personal trust required
Always structured	Normally structured
Often formal	Typically informal
Introduces learning	Sustains learning
Specific to a role or job or situation	Applicable to all contexts

Encourages adherence to procedure	Encourages self-discovery
Encourages dependency on others	Enables self-reliance
Retrospective	Future-focused

Table 1 – Training vs. coaching

1. **New information vs. existing information**

   Whereas coaching works with knowledge that people have already received or have innately acquired, training exists to give your people new knowledge for a specific purpose.

2. **External source vs. internal source**

   Training is typically provided by an external entity, e.g., a trainer, a book, a webinar, etc. Coaching is predicated on the belief that the information already exists within the person being coached.

3. **One-to-many vs. one-to-one**

   Most sales training is carried out in a group format where a trainer addresses a cohort for reasons of efficiency. On the other hand, coaching is most often delivered on an individual-needs basis.

4. **Monologue vs. dialogue**

   As training assumes the trainer is the source of knowledge, the trainer dominates communication. Coaches encourage dialogue to facilitate co-creation of a mutually agreed solution.

5. **Subject-matter expert vs. non-expert**

   To justify the primacy of expertise, the trainer is required to know more than the trainee. Coaches cultivate the expertise of the salesperson being coached, leveraging that person's knowledge.

6. **Task-focused vs. person-focused**

   Training is most often associated with transferring knowledge to engender task-specific competency. Coaching aims to develop the person who chooses which competency to apply.

7. **One-off vs. continuous**

Once training has been delivered and learning transfer has been evaluated, it usually ends. Coaching strives to achieve continuous improvement throughout the salesperson's tenure.

8. **No trust vs. trust**

In general, coaching requires mutual trust and openness if the coaching relationship is to pay dividends. Training merely requires cognitive attention and a willingness to engage in the session.

9. **Structured vs. unstructured**

Training delivers learning in a logical, sequential manner to bring a person from novice to competent. Coaching is dynamic in so far as it addresses needs as they occur at any point.

10. **Formal vs. informal**

Training takes the form of a master-student relationship where the student recognizes the superiority on the side of the trainer. Coaching engenders equality between coach and coachee.

11. **Introducing learning vs. sustaining learning**

Training provides knowledge in order to meet learning objectives. Coaching follows this process by embedding this knowledge, ensuring it is applied and that training investment is protected.

12. **Specific context vs. multiple contexts**

By its nature, sales training provides learners with knowledge for specific contexts. In contrast, coaching is flexible in that it adopts a framework which can be applied in almost any context.

13. **Procedure vs. self-discovery**

Training requires learners to follow the system, process or methodology being demonstrated. Coaching encourages the salesperson to master what they have learned by adopting it and improving it.

14. **Dependency vs. self-reliance**

Coaching requires the coachee to think for themselves and to develop a personal response to challenges. Training on its own risks dependency on the trainer, manager or the source of knowledge.

15. **Retrospective vs. perspective**

While training works based on a systematic approach that has achieved past results, coaching is focused on potential and the future results which can be achieved.

Coaching Self-Assessment

Read the statements below to gauge how prepared you are to coach your team. Circle the relevant number on the right-hand side. 1 = I have work to do. 5 = I have mastered this skill.

Part 1 Coaching Skills   **Self Score**

1	I understand the core principles of coaching	1 2 3 4 5
2	I feel confident about my ability to coach my team	1 2 3 4 5
3	I know how to apply coaching to get results from people	1 2 3 4 5
4	I know who in my team needs coaching and why	1 2 3 4 5
5	I dominate the listening, not the talking	1 2 3 4 5
6	I show curiosity and learn from each contributor's viewpoint	1 2 3 4 5
7	I ask questions which get my people to think for themselves	1 2 3 4 5

Part 2 Coaching Proactively   **Self Score**

1	I make time to coach my people on a regular basis	1 2 3 4 5
2	I have a coaching plan for individuals and the team as a whole	1 2 3 4 5
3	I lead 1:1s and team meetings using a coaching style	1 2 3 4 5
4	I take advantage of opportunities in everyday situations	1 2 3 4 5
5	I leverage the innate creativity of my team to find solutions	1 2 3 4 5
6	I find ways to align people's goals with business goals	1 2 3 4 5

| 7 | I know my people's strengths and areas for development | 1 2 3 4 5 |

Part 3 Coaching Reactively   Self Score

1	I can recognize when my people are stuck	1 2 3 4 5
2	I encourage autonomy and self-reliance	1 2 3 4 5
3	I know when to hold back and when to intervene	1 2 3 4 5
4	I keep accountability on the salesperson's side of the table	1 2 3 4 5
5	I guide my people to learn from difficult situations	1 2 3 4 5
6	I facilitate the discovery of lessons from challenges	1 2 3 4 5
7	I ensure that I follow up after coaching sessions	1 2 3 4 5

Acknowledgments

Zeeshan Hafeez, Chief Revenue Officer, VeeOne Health; Rakhi Voria, Vice President, IBM Global Digital Sales Development; Tim Wood, Sales Director Inside Sales, Intel; Giulio Magni, Sales Enablement Director Bringg; Ashton Williams, Revenue Enablement Manager, ADA Inc.; Kristen Twinning, Vice President Business Development Inside Sales, FireMon; Bob Perkins, CEO AA-ISP; Caroline McCrystal, Senior Account Manager, UK&I GTM Banking Experian; Frank Hattan, Global Head of Sales, Intertrust; John Massey, EMEA Regional Business Development VP, Commercial Sales & Channel SAP; John Carr, Head of Inside Sales, IFS; Sheena Badani, Senior Director of Marketing, Gong.io; Billy Franz, Director Emerging Business & Channel, SADA; Murray Cowell, Partner CCF; Adrian Foley, Global Head of Sales, Teamwork.com; Jonathan Swartz, Director Azure Sales, Microsoft, Carol Rossi, Senior Leader Field Communications, NetApp; Alejandro García Machuca, Global Learning Business Partner, Customer Success Change Team, SAP; Nick Feeney, AVP Commercial Sales, MURAL; Brian Signorelli, VP, GTM Vendr; Pradeepa Kolli, Head of Global SDR/Inside Sales, Workplace @Facebook; Andrew Tilling, CEO The Hive; Sindre Halland, CEO, SalesScreen; Axel Lagerborg, VP Worldwide Sales, Sorted Group; Joe Venuti, Vice President Sales Development, Upkeep; Bill Parry, Director Sales Enablement, Privitar; Emma Maslen, Vice President and General Manager, EMEA & APAC Ping Identity; Mike Weinberg, Author, *Sales Management Simplified*; Pete Starr, Managing Director, Chilli; Dustin Abney, Enterprise Sales Manager, U.S. East Redgate Software; Ryan McNitzky Sales Director AMER Enterprise Accounts - Redgate Software; Per Anders Åberg, Manager Business Development, Nordics Salesforce; Christian Curdy, Regional Sales Manager, Onfido; Steve Catchpole, Global Sales Enablement Manager, Redgate Software; Lori Harman, Vice President, Global Digital, Virtual and Renewal Sales NetApp; Alison, Shell, and the team at Practical Inspiration Publishing. Sophie and the team at Newgen Publishing.

My parents, Jill and Gerry, and my sisters Leah and Rachael for love and support which only a family can give. Sarah, Jack, Reilly, Murphy, Smoo for years of love, patience, and memories. Jon and Cathy, true friends. I miss you, Kate.

About the author

Mark Garrett Hayes is a sales enablement consultant, accredited Coach and certified Trainer who is truly passionate about helping sales leaders to empower their salespeople and dramatically boost both performance and revenue.

Working both in-house and remotely with sales teams internationally, Mark has developed powerful tools to help sales leaders to get the very best from their teams.

He has helped leaders reduce A-Player churn, drive greater accountability among their reps and revolutionize how they get the best from their sales people.

Mark is the host of the popular weekly *The Sales Coach* podcast where he interviews sales leaders and shares his own thoughts on getting the very best from your sales people.

Index

Note: Page locators in bold represents tables on the corresponding page